Critical Guides to French Texts

108 Gide: Les Caves du Vatican

Critical Guides To French Texts

EDITED BY ROGER LITTLE, WOLFGANG VAN EMDEN, DAVID WILLIAMS

GIDE

Les Caves du Vatican

Peter Broome

Professor of French
The Queen's University of Belfast

Grant & Cutler Ltd
1995

© Grant & Cutler Ltd
1995
ISBN 0 7293 0381 0

DEPÓSITO LEGAL: V. 4.285 - 1995

Printed in Spain by
Artes Gráficas Soler, S. A. - La Olivereta, 28 - 46018 Valencia
for
GRANT & CUTLER LTD
55-57 GREAT MARLBOROUGH STREET, LONDON W1V 2AY

For Di

Contents

Prefatory Note

All references to *Les Caves du Vatican* in this study refer to the Gallimard 'Folio' paperback edition, and appear simply in the text as a page number in parenthesis.

References to works included in the Select Bibliography bear an identifying italicized figure corresponding to the numbering in the Bibliography.

References to all other works not included in the Bibliography have full details of publication and pagination in the footnotes.

Introduction

André Gide (1869-1951) is one of the greatest question-raisers and non-conformists of modern literature: a writer of multi-layered lucidity and scrupulous self-analysis, probing hypocrisies and self-deceptions, and challenging all that is arbitrary, devious and untenable in moral attitudes. He is a vast *carrefour*. In him, established thinking of the late nineteenth century meets with the effervescence and fragmented re-evaluations of the twentieth; attachment to the symbolist aesthetic seeking pure truths beyond the realm of physical appearances meets with the sensuality of *Les Nourritures terrestres*; the Normandy puritan of ascetic severity meets with the unbridled hedonist of the Algerian journey of 1893; the incorruptible moral inquisitor meets with the tempting philosophical undercurrents of *L'Immoraliste*; the fervent believer meets with the nascent atheist; the devoted married man meets with the homosexual – in ways which pose anew questions of sincerity and deceit, self-expression and self-denial, extremism and moderation, respectability and scandal, the sedentary and the nomadic, the individualistic and the mutual, unity and duality, private man and public image. No novelist of the century has uncovered more than Gide the complexities of the self, showing that man is a simultaneity of 'sincerities' and that truth to oneself is not to sacrifice one to another or bring them to some workable compromise, but to live them to the full, in all the tension of their conflicts and polarizations. His works are the crucible of his contradictions, and find their authenticity in contradiction. They are also the record of a self believing in its inexhaustible possibilities, insatiably pursuing new equations of itself.

Les Caves du Vatican (1914) is also a *carrefour*. Published on the verge of the First World War, which was to drive a wedge into history and accelerate the crisis of values, it stands between an old and a new society. More pertinently, it stands between an old and a new Gide. 1910 sees him already looking forward to the composition of his *sotie* and its radically different manner: 'Je rêve aux *Caves*, que j'imagine écrites d'un style tout gaillard, très différent' (*2*, p.297). To which he adds: 'Lu hier à Em. ce que j'ai fait de mon roman [...] Cela est trop *nuancé*, de tons trop rompus. Quand j'écrirai les *Caves*, à côté d'un ton plat, je poserai tout net un autre ton plat' (*2*, p.322). The statements herald a break, not only from *Isabelle* (1911) to which they refer, but also from the fine filtering, the subtle gradations, the shimmering stylistic effects of *La Porte étroite* (1909), in favour of a more robust, even truculent manner, marked by more offhand, unmediated juxtapositions, testing the reader's receptivity. They also reflect a need, after an over-long immersion, to rid his system of the mollified vocabulary of sentiment and spirituality, and explore a drier, more elliptical, sharp-edged art. As he says specifically of *La Porte étroite*: 'Que j'en ai donc assez de ces tons rompus et de ces nuances fuyantes! Je rêve de personnages sans effusions, d'yeux sans larmes, de cœurs sans délicatesse. Tout le vocabulaire de l'amour m'a désaffecté pour cinq ans' (*1*, p.1550).

One should not conclude, therefore, that *Les Caves* represents a simple rebellion against an earlier style, in order to espouse a truer voice. On the contrary, Gide insists that he carried *L'Immoraliste* (1902) and *La Porte étroite*, two such antithetical works, concurrently in his mind as twins, 'l'excès de l'un trouvant dans l'excès de l'autre une permission secrète et tous deux se maintenant en équilibre' (*2*, pp.365-66): a play of 'secret permissions', counterweights and complementarities rendered all the more complex when one learns that these two works, together with *Les Caves*, formed an indissoluble creative triad in the author's mind, that one could not have existed without the other and that, had it been possible, he would have written them ideally all simultaneously (see *1*, p.1546).

The *sotie*, I would suggest, is Gide's masterpiece. Prompted by two real-life occurrences – the conversion of a freemason cousin of Emile Zola's, and the story, reported almost unnoticed in the press in 1892, of a crooked enterprise to raise money by spreading the rumour that a plot had been hatched to remove Pope Leo XIII from the Vatican throne – and adopting the deceptively superficial form of the late medieval *sotie*, a carnival of mockery, satire and fun sometimes performed during *la fête des fous*, the work expands to become an intricate mobile, holding perfectly in balance the widest possible variety of the author's artistic and psychological 'selves'. Moral insouciance and moral earnestness, detachment and *engagement*, knockabout farce and psychological refinement, elaborate charades and sincerity, affectation and naturalness, irony and lyricism, corrosive satire and youthful exhilaration, anarchical inventiveness and classical control, dispersion and concentration, surprises of chance and meticulously ordered concatenations, directness and indirectness, bluntness and subtlety, comic distraction and serious enquiry, interact and reinforce each other. It is a work which might seem stuffy in its social portrayal and archaic style, but which is disruptively modernistic in its structural mobility and stylistic play of mirrors. It is simplistic in its characterization and restricted in technique, adopting the devices of puppet-theatre, but it is richly polyphonic, echoing to unseen depths. Though the distanciation from his characters is more total than in other any work, it hides a disturbing complicity and fullness of self-observation; and the multiplication of *personnages* is such that the author, becoming nobody, fashions the most comprehensive self-portrait. It is *fictivité* pushed to such a degree that it becomes a kind of hyper-truth. Gide's true face is the sum of the false faces, all the more sincere in that irony liberates him to be none and all at once. *Les Caves du Vatican* is a novel and non-novel, defying rules and models and yet fulfilling them magnificently. One might even suggest that this paradoxical text, considered by many to be Gide's most prosaic, is the closest to a poem – if one admits the author's proposition: 'Don du poète [...] tu es le don de perpétuelle rencontre' (*1*, p.185).

1. Names and Aliases

Characterization in *Les Caves* is by no means stable. The theme of problematical identity infiltrates the work, not least in the precariousness of names. Carola forgets Julius's name when introducing her friend, so leaving the Count, already fearing the slip to literary anonymity, stranded between name and namelessness: 'Monsieur le comte...pardon! voilà que j'ai oublié votre nom!' (p.52). He fares no better with Lafcadio, even when doing his own introductions: 'Mais permettez d'abord que je me nomme [...] il tira de son gilet une carte et la tendit à Lafcadio, qui la posa, sans la regarder, sur la table' (p.58): a snub to a man unsure of the 'réalité de sa penseé' who now has these credentials discarded as irrelevant. When Lafcadio later picks up the card, murmuring *'Comte Julius de Baraglioul...Dapprima importa sapere chi è'* (p.60), he broaches the question of knowing who a person is, despite official labels, a question lit by the switch to Italian, which binds the linguistic and psychological games of hide and seek. He then consults Julius's entry in the 'dictionnaire des contemporains' or *Who's Who?* Lafcadio has a set-back to *his* nominal pretentions when, armed with a visiting-card bearing his new alias 'Lafcadio de Baraglioul', he is told that no such person exists. And, in tearing the card in half and throwing 'Lafcadio' down one drain and 'Baraglioul' down another, he illustrates the rift in the self, the suspect soldering of parts, and the way in which, invisibly, they may join in some underground stream.

The uneasy marriage of names sprouts in the text. Arnica, stuck with her botanical label, yearns to be free under another name, envies her sister's elegant title, and agonizes over her own choice of partner, caught between unacceptable pairings: 'Arnica Blafaphas?... Arnica Fleurissoire? incapable de décider entre l'atrocité de ces deux noms' (p.113). The fusion, or confusion, of names re-emerges in the portmanteau nickname of the inseparables, Fleurissoire and Blafaphas, *les Blafafoires*: a humorous conjunction (a 'malheur conjugal' of another order), echoing the decision of the family business Lévy and Cohen to 'agglutiner les deux noms' (p.111) under the name Lévichon *and* Lafcadio's attempted family merger. And when the narrator says of the surname Blafaphas, 'celui qui écrit ces lignes a pû voir un Blaphaphas, notaire, un Blafafaz coiffeur, un Blaphaface charcutier, qui, interrogés, ne se reconnaissaient aucune origine commune...' (p.110), this is not simply a piece of mock-philological or genealogical erudition. It is a comment on names that do not hold true to themselves but blur at the edges, on divergences and disunities within the same, on people not recognizing their similarities, and on the theme of family links and common origins (like those shared by Julius and Lafcadio).

The deceptiveness of identity-cards 'deconstructs' psychology. Protos's appearance as 'undercover agent' is mirrored by his card: 'L'inconnu se recommandait du cardinal André, ainsi que l'attestait la carte de celui-ci [...] la carte était sous enveloppe' (p.93): credentials as covert as those of another authoritative (or authorial) André in the wings (whom does *he* vouch for and how reliably?). What *credit* one gives to a person's bona fide status is stressed in Protos's instructions to Amédée: '*Demandez à Monsieur de Baraglioul de vous accompagner au Crédit commercial où il est connu et pourra témoigner de votre identité. Cave'* (p.182). Not only do the words 'identity' and (the Latin) 'beware' sit together here, 'agglutinés' one might say; but Protos's signature is subverted by its implicit warning-sign. In lending his rail ticket to Amédée, Julius ironically does to the sanctity of the name what Lafcadio did, disregards it as if it were interchangeable: 'Il est à mon nom; mais qu'importe' (p.183) – a double irony in that, having first testified to Amédée's identity and good *name*, he then passes him off as someone else. Amédée has undertaken his journey of 'undoing' with proof of identity tacked on his suitcase; but the departure of this nobody contrasts with the claims of the label (see p.122) and, though 'clouée', this *pièce d'identité* gives little anchorage in the vertigo of self-doubt which engulfs him.

Missing identification papers feature in the volatility of events. 'Aucun acte civil, aucun papier ne témoigne de votre identité' (p.69), Juste-Agénor tells Lafcadio. Newspaper reports of the discovery of Amédée's body draw a similar blank: '*On n'a trouvé sur lui aucun papier qui permette d'établir son identité*' (p.208). First, as his hat and suitcase vanish from the carriage, Lafcadio is glad to go incognito with no tell-tale labels: 'Bonne précaution que j'ai eue d'en enlever les initiales!' (p.196), 'Pas de papiers dans la valise; et mon linge n'est pas marqué' (p.198); but then, confusing the game of appearances which makes character a mirage, he delivers his calling card (like Protos's, 'dans une enveloppe') deliberately to Julius. Protos, cornering Lafcadio whose attachments have become 'embaraglioullées', taunts him with the nickname 'monsieur Lafcadio Lonnesaitpluski', adding 'Alors quoi, c'est donc vrai! on avait voulu s'évader?' (p.227), so reinforcing the theme, implicit in Arnica's predicament, of the name and escape. So dubbed, Lafcadio is more nonentity than identity, *personne* rather than *personnage*, falling between two, if not many, stools of personality. It is not only Amédée who, for want of a passport, borrows another name, nor Lafcadio who qualifies as 'Lonnesaitpluski'. Protos is innumerable pseudonyms, endless impersonation. 'Chanoine de Virmontal', Abruzzo bandit or 'Defouqueblize': all are subsumed by the word *Cave*, the dark hollow beneath the surface, the psychological underworld synonymous with the need to tread carefully. Ironically, Protos deludes Amédée by saying, 'Je ferais peut-être mieux de ne pas mettre mon vrai nom' (p.151). For, like layers of the onion, one would peel off one pseudonym after another to find 'Protos' at the centre, itself a pseudonym of the elusive identity. When asked early on *who* Protos was, Lafcadio can only reply, in an anticipatory reversal of roles, 'C'était un Italien, du nom de... ma foi, je ne sais plus, et peu importe!' (p.80): language slips into a vacuum between the word 'nom' and what one would swear to.

All the characters harbour another self. Upholding a single persona or living up to an image feeds its own rebel. A mere tilt can switch the poles of behaviour and re-route a personality. Armand-

Dubois, atheist and scientific free-thinker, succumbs to a latent double and, by a miraculous about-turn, becomes a meek believer. Julius de Baraglioul, tame novelist bowing to the Académie Française, is soon seen brooding on 'les étranges préoccupations qui m'habitent' (p.126); appears before Amédée most unlike himself, literally 'out of sorts', muttering thoughts in a language decidedly not 'sans détour ni mystère' (p.62); and disconcerts Lafcadio with a radical speech on the falsities of logic, order and social compromise. The virginal Fleurissoire, tucked in the backwaters of faith and fidelity, shy of life and the surprises of experience, ends up journeying, sleeping with cheap women and mixing with criminals. Even Lafcadio, with his mercurial switches between languages (themselves an alibi or alias), copes ill with a new role (see his speech to Geneviève, p.76). And who would expect him to break faith with his 'uncles' saying 'je suis Baraglioul et désormais, coquin de marquis, je te débarque de mon cœur' (p.186); or, from boyish idealist, become the world-weary cynic in a slough of *ennui*? So, as his fancy headgear flies from the train and he acquires Amédée's poor boater, Lafcadio is seen, literally and figuratively, 'wearing another hat'.

Geneviève's question of Lafcadio, 'Que vous êtes-vous laissé devenir?' (p.247), applies to all the characters. Each in turn acts out of character, becomes someone else. The recurrent verb 's'échapper' means to escape from *oneself*. Hence Amédée's startled observation of a feverish Julius: 'Ses yeux brillaient; on eût cru qu'il allait jaillir de lui-même' (p.174). And just as the flimsy pilgrim's contours dissolve in a disturbing *vaporisation du moi* – 'Le brouillard léger du matin et cette profuse lumière où s'évaporait et s'irréalisait chaque objet favorisaient encore son vertige; il s'avançait comme en un rêve, doutant de la solidité du sol [...] doutant surtout de sa présence à Rome' (p.171) – so when he joins Julius, desperate for stability, he finds the aristocrat no less *flou* and unreliable, so that no quoting of the reference book, no clutching at the label, can ward off the disintegration occurring before his eyes (see p.178). As if further to confound the *Who's Who*, Julius suffers the same existential dizziness: '... une espèce de vertige, comme si j'allais m'évaporer' (p.203). And, in stating 'Je ne me connais plus' (ibid.), he is already launched in the same direction which will lead Lafcadio to be redefined, or undefined, as 'Monsieur Lonnesaitpluski'.

With Julius unable to recognize himself, Amédée also finds him unrecognizable, no matter how obstinately he chants the name: 'Alors Fleurissoire eut un doute [...] Julius, Julius lui-même, ce. Julius auquel il parlait, Julius à quoi se raccrochait son attente et sa bonne foi désolée, ce Julius non plus n'était pas le vrai Julius' (p.178). In a book with so many stand-ins and substitutions – Julius acts as Anthime's proxy at the Vatican, Amédée travels on Julius's ticket, Julius asks Lafcadio (with wonderful irony) to go in his place to retrieve Amédée's body from Naples, the Holy Father has been replaced by the unauthorized version, and Anthime suggests that even God, whatever name He goes under, 'Monsieur le Principal' or 'l'Etre suprême', has been switched – one has doubts about whom one has seen and is now dealing with. Hence Amédée's problem with a cryptic *Qui?*: ' – Alors, vous l'avez vu? dit-il [...] – Qui? demanda Julius. Ce *qui?* retentit en Amédée comme un glas' (p.174), and his inability to clarify another 'Lonnesaitpluski', the one at the heart of one's faith.

The failure to recognize someone for who or what he is structures the *sotie*. Amédée has to look twice at Julius, Julius fails to see Lafcadio as murderer, and Lafcadio does not detect Protos in Defouqueblize. Juste-Agénor suggests to Lafcadio that his and Julius's identities should remain unknown to each other: 'je crois qu'il vaut mieux que vous ne vous... reconnaissiez pas' (p.71), the hesitation over the verb signalling its key value. Of the Marquis de Gesvres, Lafcadio says, 'il prêtait une attention particulière aux chaussures, par quoi se reconnaissent les gens [...] aussi sûrement et plus secrètement que le reste du vêtement et que par les traits du visage' (p.88), so implying that one recognizes people, problematically, through half-hidden or peripheral details and in the most unlikely places. Protos's distinction between *crustacés* and *subtils* hinges on the issue of recognition, highlighted by its sharp formulation: 'Nos copains tenaient pour admis ces axiomes: 1° Les subtils se reconnaissent entre eux. 2° Les crustacés ne reconnaissent pas les subtils' (p.228). And the same verb echoes, reflexively, through Amédée's soul-searching: 'Comment s'y reconnaître à présent?' (p.170): how to see one's way clearly, or recognize oneself?

References concerning greater or lesser degrees of likeness further destabilize character. We learn how Baldi, expert in mimicry, 'se départait de toute ressemblance avec lui-même' (p.85); and Protos's philosophy, underlying his elastic features which could 'exprimer n'importe quoi', was that 'dans ce monde, il importait de n'avoir trop l'air de ce qu'on était' (p.87). The new-style Julius and the travestied Defouqueblize expound on a similar theme: the courage needed to shed acquired images of ourselves and defy resemblances. 'Nous vivons contrefaits, plutôt que de ne pas ressembler au portrait que nous avons tracé de nous d'abord' (p.204), says one, while the other deplores the constraints of that 'image de nous [...] qui ne nous ressemble que fort peu' (p.225). Lafcadio also plays up to an image: 'je n'ai guère l'air Baraglioul! Nous tâcherons [...] de nous faire plus ressemblant' (p.63); and in reply to Juste-Agénor's exclamation, 'Dieu merci! c'est à sa mère qu'il ressemble', the illegitimate son's words are left in the air, as a tantalizing blank, a kind of 'watch this space': '– Si je ne laisse pas trop paraître, m'est-il tout à fait défendu de ressembler aussi à ...' (p.69). Amédée, arriving in Rome, is snared by deceptive similarities: first assuming that he is mistaken for someone else when hailed by a woman in gaping dressing-gown; and then fancying a gratuitous resemblance with a comforting figure from back home (see pp.137, 138). And Protos (a never-ending play of appearances) kids the innocent that he alone can see the resemblance between San-Felice and Bardolotti, and therefore between two non-existences, since both are aliases.

That a person's singularity is so easily dispersed in likenesses raises the question: what belongs to whom? Just as Amédée accumulates bits and pieces of other people – Lafcadio's cast-off mistress, her cufflinks, Julius's rail ticket and, in a final grab, Lafcadio's beaver hat – so Lafcadio sees his possessions, from a piece of skin from his ear to his stolen suitcase, vanishing from the train. On this journey of dispossession, props and costumes have a natural tendency to change hands. The short-sighted Defouqueblize inadvertently (though with a *cave*at) drinks Lafcadio's champagne instead of his own Saint Galmier. And the opening of private mail, whether Lafcadio's *carnet* by Julius, Amédée's letters by Protos, or the *poste restante* of a M. Gaspard Flamant by Lafcadio ('que j'ai été réclamer comme mienne', p.187), extends the network concerning 'properties', misappropriation, identities not safe within their own frontiers, and the general penetrability of psychology.

Indeed, is any character self-contained? Like the confidential story which, once released by Protos, cannot stay within bounds, psychology spills between persons. The *dramatis personae*, clearly categorized from the outset – atheist versus believer, scientist versus artist, socialite versus church mouse, stay-at-home versus adventurer, pillar of the establishment versus subversive, innocent versus trickster – redefine themselves in the light of shared or exchanged characteristics. It is not simply that all have a psychological *lacune*, or missing person, by whom each in turn is undermined. They also acquire the traits, as well as the possessions, of other persons, in interreflections so mobile that one cannot hold the line. Fixing his tie, Anthime props up a fragment of mirror and 'se pencha vers son propre reflet' (p.15). The street-walking Lafcadio, passing 'devant la glace d'une devanture' (p.63), queries his image. Before his demise from the train, Amédée tries to fix his reflection against a moving background: 'chercha comme Narcisse sur l'onde, sur la vitre, à distinguer du paysage son reflet' (p.194); and, in a flicker of illuminated squares projected on the embankment among which dances 'l'ombre falote de Fleurissoire', the last image is of a man trying vainly to 'get things straight': 'Sur le fond de la vitre, à présent noire, les reflets apparaissaient plus clairement. Fleurissoire se pencha pour rectifier la position de sa cravate' (p.195). In these makeshift mirrors, wavering, broken or obscured, what one sees is less a match between the character and himself than with someone else. So, as Amédée leans towards this inadequate mirror-image of himself, the reader perceives an almost perfect one ('se pencha ... cravate'), at a lucid distance, of Anthime. It is as he agonizes over donning Amédée's shabby coat, in a reluctant swapping of appearances, that Lafcadio scrutinizes himself in the mirror: 'penché sur le lavabo, il commença de s'examiner dans le miroir' (p.197) – again to an accompaniment of flashing effects of light ('une file de lumières passa derrière la vitre dépolie du closet') half-obliterating the visible identity. Whom, then, does one see in the mirror? Apart from Lafcadio vaguely seeing himself, one sees other likenesses: Anthime and Amédée in the same posture ('se pencha ...penché'), and caught in the frame of identical patterns of reference ('cravate ... faux col ... vitre ... lumière'), where the verb 'pencher' implies a tilting from the perpendicular (or off 'the straight and narrow') towards the *abîme* of a decentralized self.

Lafcadio, devoted to uniqueness, suffers the most encroaching of mirror-images: a full-scale portrait penned by Julius. And in musing 'ça m'aurait plu d'avoir un frère' (p.187), how could he foresee that it would be this clinging double or Siamese twin, stealing his psychology and his cherished *acte gratuit*? The half-brothers are, for a moment, virtually one and the same person, extensions of a single thought. And when Lafcadio, viewing Amédée on the train, distances himself with the contemptuous 'Entre ce sale magot et moi, quoi de commun? (p.189), he cannot imagine the complexity of the answer, which goes far beyond cufflinks, common acquaintances and family connections. For on a deep psychological level they, too, are echoes of each other: both have seen their lives take a new turn with a tingle of excitement (see pp.63, 119); but both undergo a 'change of life' crisis and lose their way, with the same uncertainties as to who they are, the same nostalgia to rejoin old playmates, and the same craving for a stable vision of things instead of the nightmare of appearances which has swamped them. Hence, in throwing Amédée from the train, is not Lafcadio throwing out his own image? And in wondering if he should hide the victim's coat under his own, is he not divulging the extent to which he already wears two coats one under the other, *l'endroit* and *l'envers* of the same psychology? As Gide once said of himself: 'Je ne suis qu'un petit enfant qui s'amuse, doublé d'un

pasteur protestant qui l'ennuie' (*2*, p.250). The mirror in which one
would not expect to see Lafcadio is Armand-Dubois: willowy free
spirit as opposed to crusty dogmatist. Though unknown to each
other, their meeting of minds is extensive, however. 'Je veux, si je
guéris, n'en être obligé qu'à moi-même' (p.29), snorts Anthime.
Lafcadio has the same fear of indebtedness, saying 'vous ne pourrez
m'amener à me sentir votre obligé' (p.77). Reading the last
epigraph, 'Only one thing alone can cure us from being ourselves!',
one sees that the two are drawn, from opposite ends of the
psychological spectrum and the text, to serve the common theme of
cure, physical or spiritual, while reflecting ironically on the
characterization of a book where individuals have great difficulty in
being themselves. Lafcadio, then, is not entirely 'his own man'; and
the characters are vastly 'indebted' to each other. The self-
deceptions of Anthime's *libre pensée* illuminate Lafcadio's own;
and in the aftermath of their two rebellious gestures, the desecration
of the Madonna or the *acte gratuit*, Anthime's chastened thoughts
speak for both: 'aboutir à ce dérisoire attentat' (p.34). And each has
an 'apparition' which, sacred or profane, Virgin or Geneviève,
seems the same, uniting first and last, and showing that the sharpest
antitheses can be portraits of each other.

The book is, in unusual senses, a literary *Who's Who*. It is not
only in the merged businesses of Lévy and Cohen that one can
'agglutiner les deux noms'. Nor is it only Julius who might say 'ne
pas ressembler au portrait que nous avons tracé de nous d'abord'
(p.204). For Gide, too, takes the luxury of escaping from his own
models, establishing the terms of character only to belie them, so
testing the credibility of the notion of *personnage*. He traces the first
portrait all the more emphatically – techniques of caricature,
physical features set in relief as graphic summaries, details of
costume matching the man in best Balzacian tradition – the better to
dissolve it in that 'profuse lumière où s'évaporait et s'irréalisait
chaque objet' (p.171). It is in this way, in denying their own
simplicity, that the characters illustrate Gide's statement made
during the composition of *Les Caves*: 'Mes personnages, que je ne
voyais d'abord que fantoches, s'emplissent peu à peu de sang réel'

(*2*, p.377); and his belief, eroding from within that of Anthime, that psychology cannot be compartmentalized or reduced to a simplistic divisionism. For who is to say, despite Lafcadio's rejection of what he sees as a 'Belle collection de marionnettes [dont] les fils sont trop apparents' (p.188), that a *crustacé* is not a hidden *subtil*?

Another name underwrites the text, that of Gide: a name, one might think, which needs no identification papers. Yet how is Gide translated into the book? How many aliases does he assume? How does one recognize him? 'De connaître un peu vos amis m'apprendrait peut-être à vous connaître' (p.80), says Julius to the heterogeneous Lafcadio. Could one not say the same of the author? One might be tempted to see a special relationship, the closest reflections, between Gide and Lafcadio: that prodigal son who seeks independence outside family ties, whom the narrator addresses as 'Lafcadio, mon ami'. The dating of events, in the early 1890s, and the mention of the boy's 'merveilleux voyage en Algérie', described as 'le meilleur temps de ma vie' (p.87), make an inviting link between art and life, invoking Gide's North African journeys of 1893. At a finer intratextual level, one might see a telling likeness between Lafcadio's variable handwriting and vocal flexibility and those exercised, in parallel, by the author himself. For when we learn that 'il écrivit, au crayon d'une grande écriture cabrée, très différente de la première' (p.59), we are reminded not only of the variety of Gide's voices from one literary work to the next, none of which seems capable of containing the expressive pliabilities of the self, but also the chameleon-like style of this one, with its changes of register and 'catch-me-if-you-can' dexterity. And, in watching on Lafcadio's face 'un sourire qui n'avait rien d'hostile; il semblait plutôt amusé, mais ironique' (p.57), one sees identical smiles: one within the fiction, and one presiding stylistically over the fiction, superimposed as one.

But the narrator, Gide's proxy, has no exclusive kinship with the youth. It, too, is the property of others. For Julius and Protos also say, 'Lafcadio, mon ami'. Alliances and adoptions are not so simple. Indeed, does not Gide find a more faithful reflection in Julius: the intellectual novelist, with a compulsive appetite for moral debate, haunted by the father-figure, testing his hidden tendencies on paper, whose experimental character is a replica of Lafcadio? Or in Protos: who can take any form, become any character, put on virtuoso performances the better to deceive, the literary impostor synonymous with doubt and a crisis of faith? Or in Amédée: the timorous puritan, the straight-laced God-fearing introvert of Gide's youth, destined to go on a journey which will throw spiritual issues into requestion? Or even, since he is the common progenitor of the divergent strains Julius and Lafcadio, in Comte Juste-Agénor? Or perhaps in the congregation of Lafcadio's 'uncles', those pseudo-relatives at a further remove who do not appear in the book, but whose formative influences feed psychology from afar, bringing together spontaneity and 'calcul', urge and restraint, urbanity and naturalness, premeditation and play? The name 'Gide' is dispersed among all such *alter egos*, in a play of mirrors more intricate than that which binds the characters. And, whereas in *La Porte étroite* or *L'Immoraliste*, personal experience was channelled, however indirectly, through a single character, Jérôme or Michel, here in *Les Caves* one seeks Gide via innumerable complex routes, through shifting patterns of appropriation, substitution, identification and disguise, and from different degrees of distance, among a host of literary cousins several times removed.

There is a final alias: that of the book as *sotie*. Is it simply a novel under another name? And, if so, what are *its* family links and likenesses? Like Protos, modern version of the mythical Proteus, the text is a master of *travestissement*, casually adopting innumerable styles and guises: encyclopedic inserts *à la Balzac*, phases of theatrical dialogue, cloak and dagger suspense, mock-Victorian melodrama, romanticized heart-fluttering. And into its mosaic are incorporated all kinds of texts and textual codes: newspaper cuttings, extracts from periodicals, jottings from diaries, cryptic mottos, various letters, literary quotations, and assorted epigraphs from different sources in different languages. The *sotie* is not confined to a single genre or a single set of habits of behaviour. Like Gide it is legion, and its literary identity equally problematical.

2. Openings and Closures

Doors are a compulsive motif. Anthime's scientific world is one of limited access where, even for his wife, it is agreed that 'il livrerait passage' (p.11) at fixed hours. The Armand-Dubois's flat is all doors and introverted 'little boxes' (see p.22). The resemblance to Anthime's maze, with its 'compliqué système de boîtes à couloirs [...] à portes de couleurs ou de formes différentes' (p.13), some leading somewhere and some not, is not gratuitous. Nor is Véronique's 'forced entry' into her husband's experiments and that of the Virgin Mary into the atheist's bedroom. This visitation has its prelude: Julie seen, like a luminous icon, through a half-open door over the threshold of which Anthime casts a mocking remark. And as the reader slips from one chapter to the next, invited to 'passer outre', attention shifts to other doors, leading beyond the rational: 'Cette nuit Anthime eut un songe. On frappait à la petite porte de sa chambre; non point à la porte du couloir [...] on frappait à une autre porte dont, à l'état de veille, il ne s'était pas jusqu'alors avisé' (p.35). That this is a psychological door, a sliding panel of the mind, is shown by the blurring of outer and inner: 'il sentit à la fois qu'il était sans résistance et que la porte allait céder'. Julius will soon feel excitement at 'la porte du douze', Lafcadio's address, caught between a *morale fermée* and a *morale ouverte*; and as he reaches the corridor, flanked by 'des portes closes' (p.50), he hesitates – as do we, in a moment of contrived suspense – at a half-open one with its ray of light, through which he is led by his female door-opener, Carola. He suffers the stimulus and frustration of door again on visiting the Pope, passing from antechamber to antechamber without seeing the object of his mission – an image of the religious quest, where no door opens on the truth, as at the Castel Sant'Angelo with its figurative 'No entry' sign, access being granted only to 'les voyageurs munis de cartes' (p.145), those proof against conflicts and inconsistencies of identity.

Reference to the opening and closing of doors frequently marks 'thresholds' of the text, new paragraphs or ends of chapters, where events and personal evolutions are about to take a new turn. Having burned his books, Lafcadio stands by a window in self-purification before stepping into the street. And at the end of Part Two, he waits for ten minutes at an open door, an expectancy relieved by the news of Juste-Agénor's death and the breaking of the paternal link. '– Allons! se disait-il en regagnant l'impasse Claude Bernard, le moment est venu. *It is time to launch the ship*' (p.91): a linking of impasse and release which stresses the theme of directions, which go where and which are blind alleys. Confiding in the Comtesse, Protos says ironically (for he is the very spirit of the door and no-one is more adept at finding exits and escape-routes): '... le nombre des portes m'effraie' (p.94). For those used to more linear lives, however, the words are ominously true: an excess of doors can be dangerous to your health. Like Anthime's Virgin, Protos appears and vanishes by a previously unnoticed door, a panel below Carola's bed. The crucial encounters of Amédée's confused pilgrimage are signalled by uncontrollable movements of the door: not only the bewildering exits and entrances of Protos, but, thanks to a faulty lock, the intrusions of Carola, in another 'other-worldly' bedroom visitation, not so spiritual. In a nice transfer of roles, Amédée will make his own entry *à la Protos*, through a sliding door into Lafcadio's railway compartment; and it is at the door of the carriage that his battle of life and death, salvation or perdition, occurs, and he is forced, literally, to 'passer outre'. His last gesture – 'sa main gauche agrippa le cadre lisse de la portière' (p.195) – is symbolic of the man striving to keep his life within a frame, in a world where doors have become his enemy. (Like Lafcadio, Gide manipulates the lock at this point: at the close of one chapter his 'hero' is fingering the 'double fermeture', the textual space yawns wide, and at the beginning of the next Amédée is swinging in the void.) Previously, Lafcadio has recalled an escapade with 'oncle Wladi', a recollection dominated by images of corridors and doors, all the more suggestive, in an atmosphere of involuntary memory and dream. of Freudian passageways of the mind which spring subliminal traps. The door-knob is a hypnotic object: 'Sa chambre est à l'extrémité d'un couloir [...] La poignée de cuivre de sa porte, en forme de tête de lion, est retenue par un gros clou' (p.190). And as Wladi, his bedside 'apparition', leads him on a forbidden journey (to wine flask rather than Holy Grail), all the pleasures and perils of the quest hinge on the imminent opening of doors: 'Devant la porte de sa mère, tous deux s'arrêtent [...] Quelles précautions devant la porte du salon!' (p.191). Just before opening the latch to eject Amédée, Lafcadio fancies that the wretch might be intent on rifling his case: a case now permanently open as he lost the key and had to have the lock forced. Amédée, one remembers, had trouble with the 'pène de la serrure' of his bedroom and is, at that instant, struggling to fix a stud, like a miniature door-knob, into a recalcitrant shirt collar. Even Lafcadio is nearly dragged out (see p.196), feeling the pull of opposites at this dangerous frontier. It is a mark of character and the routes they will choose that we see Julius retreating into 'une nuit de bon sommeil derrière une porte solidement verrouillée' (p.213), while Lafcadio lies, open to all visitations, behind 'la porte, que jamais il ne ferme la nuit' (p.245). One might see, in the proliferation of doors, a self-parodic reference to *La Porte étroite* and its implication of a single door ('Strait is the gate') at the end of a narrow road of spiritual endeavour. They reflect the multidirectional structure of the book, emphasizing the hidden corridors of the self, the inadequacies of monocular vision, and a view of reality as innumerable divergent possibilities.

References to windows, open, half-open or closed, complement the pattern. Amédée plunges into a stifling world, where his plea 'Ouvrez un peu la fenêtre' (p.138) does little to clear his existential thick head. After closing the carriage door, Lafcadio feels boxed in: '"On manque d'air ici". Il ouvrit la fenêtre' (p.196). Julius, Amédée and Lafcadio are all seen standing by open windows overlooking gardens. For Julius, the embassy lawns create a 'clean' zone which holds the scruffiness of life at bay (p.45). And Amédée can only admit a small dose of reality: 'Il laissait la fenêtre ouverte; non toute grande assurément [...] mais un des battants rabattu de manière que ne lui parvinssent pas directement les effluves' (p.132). It is left to Lafcadio, finally, to transcend his fever and steep himself in the regenerative offerings of the world at large, savoured now through a fully opened window looking out, not on a half-dark as with Julius and Amédée, but to admit 'par la fenêtre grande ouverte, l'aube où frissonne un arbre du jardin' (p.249).

   Les Caves is full of alcoves and enclosures, other than the 'cachots' of the Vatican, symbolic of repressions beneath the faith. The growth on Anthime's neck has its own secret retreat, the pocket in his collar: 'une sorte d'alvéole réservée cachait la loupe, et la révélait à la fois' (p.16) – an attempted 'censorship' which advertises the abnormality as it tries to conceal it. The cyst has grown since its discovery by Véronique, 'comme si, démasquée, la grosseur n'avait plus à garder de retenue' (ibid.): an image of the power of expansion of what one denies and how dissimulation stores up its revenge. Even the Madonna's stucco hand, transferred from its original niche or 'retrait' into the iconoclast's waistcoat, finds its way out in a miraculous revelation, by which the closet believer is revealed to himself. News of his conversion leaks out like other secrets in the book, no matter how often people swear silence or Protos puts finger to lips in a 'hush-hush' job. And like Anthime's 'loupe', tucked in its cell, the disclosure of the pent-up Pope expands beyond measure. Lafcadio's private drawer has a wax seal. It, too, is broken, and soon afterwards Lafcadio decides inexplicably to 'give himself a break' and divulge his life-story to a stranger. People's personal mail is tampered with: a further breaking of seals. And one of Blafaphas's quirkish inventions is 'un verrou de sûreté pour son pupitre, qui du reste ne contenait pas plus de secrets que son cœur' (p.112): as empty as the compartments for rats which hold nothing, or the Vatican cellars where the Pope is supposedly locked away.

   The text evolves tantalizingly between closure and disclosure. Carola's costume after Amédée's death, subdued yet over-showy, captures the balance: 'Le manteau noir la *recouvrait* [...] son chapeau tumultueux [...] la *signalait*' (p.213, my emphasis). As, too, does the image of the 'widow' who attracts Lafcadio: a model of decency who, for a split second, lifts her skirt to give a glimpse of leg and red stocking. And where do Lafcadio's revelations lie between a genuine need to divulge, and a willed 'press-release' to 'épater le bourgeois'?

The characters of the comic gallery all lead confined lives. Anthime 'sortait peu' (p.14): immobilized by lumbago, and entrenched in a scientific dogmatism. Though flattering himself that, as novelist, no human experience is foreign to him, Julius 'était peu descendu jusqu'à présent hors des coutumes de sa classe' (p.49), safe in a social and literary cocoon. He, like Anthime, returns with relief to the sanctity of his den, where life's embarrassing elements, including one's own desires, are distilled into their harmless fictional equivalent. Amédée, like Arnica whose 'âme inéclose' (p.110) hid in the bosom of Mme Semène, has lived 'sous tutelle' (p.128). Nor can he do without protective coverings, scarf or overcoat, for fear of fluctuations of temperature (see p.112). Hence the distinction between *crustacés* and *subtils*: the *crustacés* carrying with them their shells or shelters, self-enclosed, slow-moving, hardened to change. If the *subtil* of Protos's formula is versatile and pliable, never showing the same face twice, then conversely the *crustacé* is stolidly true to himself, resistant to the fitful mutations of living reality. And whereas *subtils* come in endless fine shadings, the *crustacés* close ranks to form one 'unique grande famille', so justifying Gide's famous words: 'Familles, je vous hais! foyers clos; portes refermées' (*1*, p.186). Juste-Agénor has congratulated Lafcadio on his illegitimacy, saying 'Mon enfant, la famille est une grande chose fermée' (p.70). Anthime, Julius and Amédée have never left the House nor negated the authority of the father. Unlike her sisters who spent the year between Pau and Tarbes, Arnica 'demeurait, été comme hiver, près du père' (p.108) and is now a stunted flower. Amédée, we learn, 'n'avait d'autre ambition que de succéder à son père' (p.112). Julius has also shadowed the father, writing *his* life-story, closing the family circuit. Even Anthime the free-thinker is obsessed by 'Monsieur le Principal', and it is not inconsistent that he should scuttle under the roof of the Church, the House of the Father, as much a victim of 'la crainte quasi superstitieuse' (p.101) as pious Amédée.

Lafcadio, by contrast, is the prodigal son: free from family ties, brought up by occasional 'uncles' who now exert no claim. His is the model 'open' education: cosmopolitan, multi-directional, infinitely mobile. No uncle has stayed long enough to exercise a monopoly or allow one tendency to congeal at the expense of another. His unfurling *évolution créatrice* has been a process of overlaying and counterbalancing, with intellect and imagination, reason and desire, spontaneity and self-restraint, sincerity and artifice, natural impulse and aesthetic refinement, held in perfect equipoise, allowing a rare *disponibilité*. The financier Heldenbruck has inculcated, not beliefs or moral tenets, but *le calcul*, including, notably, 'des questions de change' (p.82): a quickness to translate one thing into another. Wladimir Bielkowski urges uninhibited self-expression with no postponed or repressed desire. Again the power of instant metamorphosis is stressed: 'Cet homme bizarre transforma du jour au lendemain notre existence ...' (p.84). Juggler, acrobat, illusionist, Baldi fuels the appetite for mystery and play. He teaches Lafcadio chess, as if to see life as an infinite permutation of moves; and, in calling him 'une mine inépuisable', instils the message of not stinting on the self, of not holding it in store as a treasure for some other life. A gifted mimic, he shows the *subtil*'s art of becoming someone else. Faby, in encouraging his protégé to run naked by the Mediterranean, further liberates him from moral self-consciousness and prudery. And the Marquis de Gesvres, who spends without counting the cost, completes that education in liberality begun by Baldi: to give oneself to fitful fantasies rather than utilitarian needs, the former being the least recoverable expressions of the self. The 'uncles' have been birds of passage. 'Jette mon livre et quitte-moi', the 'disciple' is told in *Les Nourritures terrestres* (*1*, p.250). Lafcadio, by natural good fortune, will absorb their successive lessons and leave his educators behind.

Protos might be counted as a sixth 'uncle'. His influence is an obscure liberation (see p.81). He, too, is an overnight transformer. Asked what he is doing there, his reply is 'je prends mon élan' (p.87). Not held by a status quo but gathering momentum towards a new one, he is the energy of *devenir*. His catch-phrase, 'qu'à cela ne tienne', shows that nothing is an immovable obstacle; and spoken by Lafcadio like an 'Open Sesame', it has enabled him to PASSER OUTRE and flee the gaol where he, like the Pope, was only a false version of himself.

Lafcadio and Protos are agents of disturbance. Their presence assures the dialectic between *crustacés* and *subtils*, closure and openness, stasis and change. As is the Madonna to the quantified world of Anthime, so is the bohemian Lafcadio to the starchy decorum of Julius, and the kaleidoscopic Protos to Amédée's homely order. It is not that cracks have not appeared in the respective closed fronts. For, just as the first chapter shows marital tensions, so, within the individual, one detects incompatibilities in the pretended unity of the self, which is also an institutionalized partnership: an uneasy compromise between oneself and a number of 'better halves' living under one roof. Anthime's persona crumbles under the weight of prayers and candles. Because of his book's bad press and Juste-Agénor's dismissal of it (rejection by the Father), Julius wavers as a self-assured value (p.47). The Pope's kidnap stirs similar doubts and divides Amédée from himself (p.119). But it is the encounter with Lafcadio or Protos which widens the breach, aggravating the *mise en éveil* to a critical degree.

The journey represents the act of 'coming out'. It is a venture which tests, in Protos's words. 'qu'on n'a rien d'insolite en soi, qui demanderait à sortir' (p.225). How does one go equipped into the unknown? 'Tu n'as rien de prêt' (p.121), says Arnica as Amédée goes off without prior arrangements or protective wraps. It is a journey of 'dis-covery', stripping away preconceptions and purpose-built baggage. It is also. as Butor will suggest in *La Modification*, an exploration which redefines and invalidates the instrumentation with which one undertakes it. As characters step outside their supporting structures. they feel the vertigo of standing (perhaps for the first time) in the open. Even Protos, in bogus voice, exclaims: 'j'échappe à ma figure, je m'évade de moi ... O vertigineuse aventure!' (p.225). For Julius and Amédée, the dizziness follows the 'death' of the father, be it Count. or 'Saint-Père séquestré'. Amédée fights the battle between rest and movement, sleep and wakefulness, the journey being at odds with the deepest instincts of his nature (see p.127). His need to sleep is thwarted by attacks on the flesh, by mosquitoes, bed-bugs or Carola; and the 'insupportable démangeaison' (p.152), whether of insect-bites, retarded sexuality or spiritual unrest, becomes symbolic, so that, by the time Lafcadio comes, it is the itch of life itself and the only adequate sleep, death. Arnica's remark: 'Mais tu n'as jamais voyagé. Tu ne vas pas savoir' (p.121) is prophetic. Tormented by exits and entrances, Amédée dies from the discrepancy between openings and closure.

How one deals with the journey is a key theme. Julius's excursion into revolutionary conjectures is temporary: he soon rejoins the accepted order and the reassurance of never having changed – a move mirrored in advance by his daughter who, seeing Lafcadio, 'avait regagné en grande hâte la demeure paternelle' (p.76). Anthime, too, has enough of unfulfilled expectations, tall stories and hypotheses, and retreats to his world of solids, secure links and determinable cause and effect. The fake Defouqueblize exclaims: 'Mon Dieu! mon Dieu! qu'est-ce que je vais devenir?... Si je retournais tout de suite à mon compartiment?' (p.221) – words which Anthime's rats might echo. Amédée longs to leave the labyrinth for the security of home, a desire picked up in many references: Protos's advice not to look back en route, 'et ne vous retournez pas non plus' (p.156); Amédée's realization, in the barber's shop, that '[il] aurait dû retourner loin en arrière pour en trouver une autre' (ibid.), and, on the wrong train, that 'il dut redéfaire la route' (p.128). The epigraph to Book Two ('Julius de Baraglioul'), chiming with Gide's title *Le Retour de l'enfant prodigue* (1907), reads: 'Il ne faut jamais ôter le retour à personne'. For Julius returns to dwell in his Father's house forever, unlike Lafcadio, who gazes unrepentant on new horizons. So, *le retour* comes to mean closing doors on disturbing questions. 'Ne cherchez pas plus loin que ce qu'on vous en dit' (p.163), Amédée was warned. Seeing his brother-in-law's sorry plight, Julius says the same: 'Le plus simple, quand on est simple, c'est de s'en tenir à ce qu'on sait' (p.234).

In the debate between openness and closure, the 'novel' itself has a key role. It is, in many ways, a 'livre ouvert'. Not only does it take family links and scatter them in all directions, so 'aerating' that 'grande chose fermée' and destabilizing a traditional pillar of society. Not only does it subvert authority and dogma via the vanishing Pope and the temporary eclipse of absolute truths. It also finds a structure which refuses causal inevitability and linear enclosure: one in which ends of chapters seal nothing but leave everything on the verge of possibilities; and where the need to go back, reawakening the hidden significances of what has preceded, is part of a continual forward process. Even in its conclusion, it is not sealed upon itself but, like Lafcadio, looks towards new prospects and new textual developments. And it does, indeed, take the form of a debate: a polarized *mise en question* of all that we assume to be true, which allows the reader no false repose. The reader, too, is 'opened up'. For, as Gide once stated: 'J'appelle un livre manqué celui qui laisse intact le lecteur'. [1]

---

[1] *Les Cahiers d'André Walter*, Gallimard, 1952, p.12.

3. Truth and Falsity

Les Caves contests conventions of truth and falsity. At its centre is the question of whether the papal seat is occupied by true or false Pope, original or impostor. Book Three was to have had as epigraph a quotation from Paul Claudel: 'Mais de quel Roi parlez-vous et de quel Pape? Car il y en a deux et l'on ne sait qui est le bon' (*1*, p.1574). Claudel, who withdrew permission for its use, could not have imagined that its absence would be so appropriate to Gide's game of hunt the thimble and the theme of missing persons. It is this centre, exploded, which scatters the word 'faux' through the work. In sowing the suspicion which acquires such vast ramifications, Protos says: 'Plus de pape est affreux, Madame. Mais [...] un faux pape est plus affreux encore' (p.99). (Which is the greater non-truth: absence of or falsity of?) The conclusion drawn by Julius from his audience is 'le pape que j'ai vu *n'est pas le vrai*' (p.237). The logical consequence should be that the Pope he did *not* see is, therefore, the true one. But, since his head was bowed, he did not actually see this one. So, the true formula should read: the Pope he did *not* see was *not* the true one. And, true or false, he did not see either. It is, ironically, Anthime, first seen as savouring a 'vaniteux plaisir de faux dieu' (p.13), who takes the next step and voices the possibility that, even on high, someone may have slipped in a phoney and that one is dealing with a 'faux Dieu'. Julius's reply dovetails nicely with the absent epigraph:

> – Et qui me dira si Fleurissoire en arrivant au paradis n'y découvre pas [...] que son bon Dieu non plus n'est pas *le vrai*?
> – Voyons; mon cher Anthime, vous divaguez. Comme s'il pouvait y en avoir deux! comme s'il pouvait y en avoir UN AUTRE. (p.238)

As in Gide's *Les Faux-monnayeurs*, the theme of the counterfeit is central. Protos first appears as 'faux prêtre'. The Fleurissoires are suspected of being 'des faux pauvres' (p.117). Amédée, knowing how events can play you false, has taken enough money to cover the possible 'faux frais...' (p.127). We learn that 'le second jour il fit un faux départ' (p.128): the suggestion being that, as Baudelaire says, 'les vrais voyageurs sont ceux-là seuls qui partent pour partir' (*Le Voyage*) and that all else is a 'faux départ'.

Vrai and *faux*, like the characters themselves, exchange identities. The fact that Protos the bogus priest, a patent fraud, convinces the Comtesse, exposes the real priesthood. Is to be milked by the Church so usual that one swallows this caricature and sees no difference? Indeed, Anthime and Véronique's treatment by the Church – 'les abus de confiance dont vous nous voyez victimes' (p.123) – is the exact image of Protos's con-trick, so that fact and fiction coincide. Protos compounds the confusion with a play of mirrors, inventing a story of copy-cat criminals cashing in on his, the true crusade. So, the arch-crook coins replicas of himself to bemuse Amédée, who never knows whether the Countess's visitor, learned of second-hand, was the authentic variety (whom we know to be false) or an impostor (whom we know to be ingenious fiction). So, the traveller chases true and false versions of what is all deception. When Protos becomes Italian peasant, Amédée assumes that only he knows the true 'priestly' face beneath. So, too, with 'Cardinal' Bardolotti: 'il fallait être bien perspicace, ou averti autant que l'était Fleurissoire, pour découvrir sous la jovialité de son air, une discrète onction cardinalice' (p.159). And as the criminals have an orgy, Amédée does not twig that their 'profane et factice gaieté' put on for a 'holy' cause is genuine, and that the 'honteuse comédie' is, for once, not staged, but real high spirits, spiced by his error.

Fact, instead of correcting, can give credence to fiction. Seeing the formalities at the Castel Sant'Angelo – identity papers, guides – Amédée finds support for his flimsy imaginings. Protos uses a press cutting exposing his deception as the means of reinforcing Amédée's trust. Julius's revelation, that 'Anthime a été joué' (p.175) and he did not *see* the Pope, strengthens the hold of

Protos's tall story. And, about to tell Anthime that the Pope is not real, Julius thinks: 'Tout de même, s'il savait que ce n'est pas au *vrai* Saint-Père qu'il doit son infortune et son exil, quelle consolation pour Armand-Dubois! quel encouragement dans sa foi!' (p.234). A notion logical and absurd: abused by the Church, to know that it is under a usurper may be a comfort to the convert; but it is a topsy-turvy reasoning which sees, in a fake Pope, a boost to one's faith! Speculating on the unmotivated crime, Julius hits on the truth of Amédée's death. But when Lafcadio reads a newspaper to prove that this *has* happened, with no motive of theft, Julius cannot cope with so much reality. He espoused it as fiction; as fact, it is too *invraisemblable* to digest. Robbed of his only explanation, he can but clutch at the remaining possibility: namely, the *truth* of Amédée's wild ramblings. Ironically, this recognition blinds him to the actual murderer before his eyes. 'Taisez-vous!' he snaps at Lafcadio, 'vous ne savez rien. Et moi qui perds mon temps près de vous dans des échafaudements ridicules' (p.210): unaware that the 'échafaudements' are the essence, while the story of crookery, though true, is a red herring. And when he says of Amédée, 'On avait peur de lui' (p.211), he is right and wrong at the same time: wrong in that it is not underground gangs who have snuffed out his brother-in-law; right in that he has stumbled on perhaps the deepest of Lafcadio's hidden motives. Carola, finally, adopting a false interpretation of the crime (looking in the wrong place for the *author*), gives Protos away to the police: showing how one can come to the wrong conclusion on the right evidence, and vice versa.

When Amédée meets Julius in Rome, a matter of life or death for the puny pilgrim, Julius merely rehearses his novel, so that 'fact' and fiction mix, and questions of Pope, Church and Lodge get tangled with story-telling. As Defouqueblize expatiates on sincerity and the deforming pressures of society, these are truths which Gide would endorse, tallying with the book's underlying message. But they are spoken through a mask. And if one denounces disguise while wearing one, does this invalidate what is said? And if society's behaviour *is* one of false fronts, then how do they differ from the charade now exposing them? Gide flirts with the paradox again in Lafcadio's visit to the tailor, where he learns of his uncle's bad debts: 'Lafcadio répugnait aux filouteries; il feignit aussitôt d'être venu précisément pour régler ces notes' (p.185). He loathes dishonesty, so he pretends! Amédée, too, is caught in a vicious circle: 'lorsque le faux prend la place du vrai, il faut bien que le vrai se dissimule' (p.180). If people have taken the false for the true, and truth, in its real guise, is spurned as an impostor, then what can it do but learn from the enemy, dress up and fight back in deceptive form? But does this not replace truth with two falsities, tarred with the same brush? Indeed, can truth compromise itself at all, a question voiced by Amédée: 'A qui se fier, sinon au pape? et dès que cette pierre angulaire cédait [...] rien ne méritait plus d'être vrai' (p.171). For if Truth is marred, nothing exists *but* falsehood. Julius's final stance is symptomatic. Faced with the riddle of the Pope, he opts out. It would be convenient if issues of truth and falsity were a simple algebraic equation: if what you have seen isn't true, then what haven't, is! He should be glad that he did *not* see the Pope, as he would have been deceived. But, seen or unseen, would not the result have been the same? Julius therefore declines to be a Sisyphus on a futile mission: 'vous venez de me dire: Halte-là! Il y a maldonne: Recommencez! Ah! non, par exemple! [...] Si celui-là n'est pas le vrai: Tant pis!' (p.178). So he retires to his own refuge of gratuitousness: truth or falsity, it's all the same.

The novel punctures pretentions to know the Truth. Armed with his master-keys, confident that behaviour is 'aisément réductible à quelques simple lois' (p.13), secure in a reality which is not refractory but operates according to a 'parfaite obéissance à l'agent', Anthime prepares his rational onslaught on the animal kingdom, to be followed by man, then God. The 'miracle' is the punishment of his simple-minded scientific pride. Amédée's notion of truth is equally naïve. His faith in its self-evident nature, his reliance on the word of authorities, is shown in his reaction to the kidnap: 'Tout le monde saurait cela, si on avait touché au Saint-Père. Ça se lirait dans les journaux' (p.119). And his desire to get to the bottom of things, unaware that it is an abyss, reflects his inability to live with the unverifiable (see p.120). Omniscience, like some paradise lost, always belongs elsewhere. 'Ces gens-là savent tout' (p.211), says Julius. And his explanation of Amédée's death boils down to one cause: 'C'est pour avoir voulu savoir qu'il est mort' (p.237). In a symbolic duet between the quest for truth and omnipresent doubt, Protos's sinister warning reverberates from the heart of the book: '– On t'en donnera, du cardinal!... C'est que, tout seul, il était fichu d'aller trouver *le vrai*!' (p.152).

Protos's apparition, unlike the Virgin's bringing faith, makes everything suspect, creating a world (perhaps like that of any novel) where all is verbal appearances and one can believe nothing. 'Je suis suspect à tous; tout m'est suspect' (p.180), moans the Existentialist fledgling, Amédée. His query, 'A qui se fier?' (p.164), sounds through all levels of the text, moral, psychological and literary. 'Eh bien! défie-toi de lui' (p.170), says Carola, advising him to mistrust the person who has warned him to mistrust. The play on the word 'Cave' highlights the irony of Amédée's predicament: 'il se défierait désormais de Cave, comme il se défiait déjà de Baptistin; et qui sait si, de Carola même ... ?' (ibid.). He will beware of 'Beware' and, in another plunge of the *mise en abyme*, may even beware of the one who has told him to beware of 'Beware'!

Variants of the verb *fier* proliferate. In whom should one confide or have confidence? Is even the word constant? Julius promises to carry out 'cette mission que vous me confiez' (p.47) and to win Lafcadio's trust, 'l'amener à confiance', albeit by dissimulation. Amédée is reassured to see soldiers at his boarding-house, 'car il avait confiance dans l'armée' (p.136). And as Protos enters, variations of the word vibrate around him (see pp.94-95) – as if 'faith' itself, by his arrival, had become disturbed, wayward and multiform. The problem of faith, via the tale of the Pope 'entre les mains des *infidèles*' (p.118, my emphasis), is at the core of the work, as it was of Gide's life. The word 'foi' passes between characters as if with no reliable owner. Of the Bishop of Tarbes, Anthime says, 'il m'a vivement encouragé dans ma foi' (p.123), through the Church has broken faith with him. Julius scolds Lafcadio, saying: 'Oh! cela vous est facile de rire, à vous qui n'entendez rien aux choses de la foi' (p.211). Even the 'faithless'

Lafcadio contracts the virus, lamenting, of the human puppet-show, that 'les fils sont trop apparents, par ma foi!' (p.188).

The *sotie* is a test of credulity, a theme seeded by Anthime's scorn for 'believers' and his own untenable position with regard to belief: 'cela me forcerait de croire à Celui qui n'existe pas' (p.29). For he is duped by his non-belief as others are by their faith. Making people believe what does not exist is the crux of Protos's enterprise, via a story defying credibility. It is relayed to the Fleurissoires: '– Vous n'allez pas y croire' (p.116). When Julius adopts the latest edition, Anthime is the incredulous listener: 'Dois-je croire à ce que vous dites?' (p.238). (A question so nagging that one applies it, too, to Gide's narration and the 'willing suspension of disbelief'.) A fine example shows how belief can sprout from what is not and feed on its own refutation. Inspecting Amédée's troublesome spot, Carola reassures him: '– Ça n'est pas ce que tu crois' (p.169). In fact, Amédée has never thought of *that*, but to find that it is *not*, now makes it a possibility, even a plausibility, gives it logical justification, even a moral necessity: he has *sinned*. And, like Anthime's *loupe*, this possibility, once let out, cannot help growing, so that Amédée repeats to Julius, 'Ce n'est pas ce que vous croyez' (p.179): an instance of *déjà vu* which makes the phrase seem like an optical illusion.

Indeed, is seeing believing? The book abounds with impediments and ailments of vision. The blind rats are not Gide's only victims. Amédée is 'un peu presbyte' (p.133). Marguerite steps off the train with 'un charbon dans l'œil' (p.22), prompting a Biblical joke on removing the mote from someone's eye (p.23). As Julius seeks moral support, he meets only his wife's glazed and soporific look (p.48). Defouqueblize drops his pince-nez and gropes about, losing grip on reality (p.219). The description as he joins Lafcadio at table is a far-reaching one: 'tenant entre deux doigts son pince-nez, il haletait dessus doucement, puis, du coin de sa serviette, il en clarifiait les verres. Lafcadio l'observait, s'étonnait de ses yeux de taupe clignotant sous d'épaisses paupières rougies' (p.220). The 'yeux de taupe' hark back to Anthime's blind animals. Trying to 'clarify the glass' reconjures Amédée looking at himself 'as through

a glass darkly'. And peering through inflamed lids recalls those of
Marguerite (p.22); as well as Lafcadio's feigning of sleep while
'watching' Amédée through closed lids, an art, significantly,
acquired from Protos: 'Protos [...] se faisait fort de reconnaître le
faux sommeil à ce léger petit tremblement des paupières ... que je
réprime en ce moment. Protos lui-même y serait pris' (p.193). Apart
from who is being taken in at this moment, for the 'Professor',
through puffy lids and pretend blindness, is the more clear-sighted,
such extracts bind the themes of interference with the eye,
deceptions practised at the frontier of the eye, and vision turned
inside out. When Lafcadio does begin to 'see through' the eye,
wondering 'si la myopie de cet homme ... [the opposite of Amédée's
defect] ...n'était pas feinte', Protos turns the tables of short-
sightedness, saying, 'c'est vous qui devriez porter des lunettes, mon
garçon; ça vous jouera de mauvais tours, si vous ne reconnaissez pas
mieux que ça les subtils' (pp.226-27). The eye plays endless tricks.
Cases disappear, a cuff-link pops up on a plate, a widow's skirt
uncovers a shapely leg. 'Je vois des espions partout' (p.153), says
Amédée, seeing imaginary followers who, unlike Lafcadio, seem to
be looking when they are not. And his resolve to keep his eyes
skinned – 'Il ouvrirait l'œil encore plus' (p.170) – is sadly self-
defeating. Protos's advice not to court attention by looking over his
shoulder but, instead, to drop a handkerchief or umbrella and 'tout
en ramassant l'objet, la tête en bas, regarder entre les jambes'
(p.154) is an arch-example of how to turn vision upside down in a
way that defeats the object (to make things look more natural), in
order to see what is not there anyway.

All characters have difficulty in seeing straight. Amédée
'commença bientôt d'y voir trouble' (p.161). Lafcadio cannot keep
words in focus as he reads the *Who's Who*: 'les lignes
tourbillonnaient devant ses yeux' (p.62). Things suffer distortion,
like the swelling of Anthime's *loupe*, when seen in a new light. A
mosquito becomes a vampire to Amédée's insomniac mind (in a
piece where the author's grandiloquent style also, by a trick of
literary perspective, makes much of little, turning a trifle into an
epic). As Defouqueblize says of champagne: 'On se fait ainsi des

monstres de bien des choses' (p.224). Before his demise, Amédée cannot 'get the lighting right' and plays with switches: from the 'éclairage trop brutal' of the compartment light to night-light to wall-lights, in fits of obscurity and illumination. The issue of Anthime's rats, and relative degrees of blindness or seeing, is picked up by Julius: 'vous ne savez donc pas quels aveugles fait de nous le respect?' (p.176).The words apply equally to the literary act: why should not we, as readers, suffer the same aberrations of vision, in a book testing to the full the fitness of the seeing eye?

More deeply, the very nature of reality is blurred and questioned. Lafcadio has had an uncle with whom 'les objets [...] perdaient poids et réalité' (p.85). By a different educative route, Amédée has the same experience: 'le brouillard léger [...] où s'évaporait et s'irréalisait chaque objet' (p.171). His attempt to crush a mosquito 'contre un tissu fuyant, vaporeux' (p.133) shows the difficulty of pinning things down against the flimsiness of reality. The barber's shop episode is a further tilt towards unsubstantiality. As he dozes off, drifting into the *inconséquence* of gratuitous thoughts, he, too, has an apparition: 'Il fermait les yeux puis, les rentrouvrant, distinguait comme dans un rêve [...] une femme aux cheveux défaits' (p.157) – a Madonna of the shampoo adverts! (Does one get the dream-woman one deserves: Anthime, a statue of Our Lady; Amédée, a voluptuous pin-up; Lafcadio, a pure family girl of good stock?) Like Sartre's Roquentin, Amédée is swamped by the senseless overspill of objects and a reality uncontrollably viscous ('substance gélatineuse ... mousse onctueuse au creux de sa main moite ...taffetas gluant'). The experience matches Lafcadio's who, on the train, also wavers between consciousness and unconsciousness. He recalls, from childhood, Wladi looming before his drowsy eyes, larger than life, wearing a nightcap 'qui l'allonge jusqu'à n'en plus finir' (p.190), and carrying a 'magic lantern' (such as enchanted Marcel in *A la recherche du temps perdu*) which lights the room 'si bizarrement que l'enfant la reconnaît à peine; elle lui paraît démesurée' (p.191), falsifying the real. It is only a step to the unreality of Amédée's death, a dizzying shadow-play, a stutter of dark and light flashes and deformed

outlines: 'On apercevait [...] danser l'ombre falote de Fleurissoire
[...] l'ombre du Chinois cabrioler' (p.194). And one more to the
dreamlike visitation of Geneviève: 'Rêve-t-il? [...] doute-t-il encore
de la réalité d'une apparition si plaisante?' (p.245). The book
borders the suspicion that all is illusion, such is the emphasis on
dream, mirages and shifting appearances. Not only do characters
not believe their eyes. They mistrust their reality, as when Amédée
sees, not Julius, but 'quelque contre-façon de vous-même' and says,
'j'ai pu douter de ma propre réalité, douter d'être moi-même ici, à
Rome' (p.181). Each catches a whiff of madness (see pp.141, 199,
211). It is a malady endemic in that journey to the brink where
reality and illusion become indistinguishable.

Gide's works all investigate sincerity. *Les Caves* has its dose
of feigned emotions: Anthime's posturing, Marguerite's histrionics,
the Comtesse's fainting fits, the theatricals of Cave and Bardolotti.
The author leads the troupe in over-acting: contrived melodrama,
hyperbole, fancy periphrasis, glossy veneers of tone which can be
wiped off the face of the text as easily as Cave's chameleon
expressions – a mocking (and self-mocking) mimicry from the
wings. The overworked handkerchief is the symbol of mock-
emotions. It is wrung, wetted, torn in anguish, pressed on hearts, as
the whole cast do their party-pieces, often covering faces in the
process (see pp.21, 94, 99, 203, 214, 245).

It is a book of *foi* and *mauvaise foi*: not simply in the sense of
contracts not honoured by the Church, superficial believers or piety
lapsing into sin, but in the Sartrean sense of self-deceit. As Protos is
denounced by Carola, so the characters are 'told on' by Gide or have
their impostures leaked. Anthime is seen to be abnormally sensitive
to what he pooh-poohs. As Lafcadio burns his photograph, a tell-
tale word reveals his fraud: 'il *se persuadait* que, ces souvenirs, il
les voyait brûler avec un contentement indicible' (p.60, my
emphasis). Julius makes a play for Carola while shedding crocodile
tears for Amédée, and his novelist's pretensions rely on 'la *flatteuse
illusion* que rien d'humain ne lui devait demeurer étranger' (p.49,
my emphasis). Even Geneviève denies the truth of her emotions: 'ne
s'avouait pas à elle-même qu'elle trouvait Lafcadio très beau'

(p.77). So many illustrations of the hoaxes perpetrated by the self on the self, of the fact that we all harbour an inner Protos, our master of disguise. And it is perhaps Protos, epitome of falsehood, who stays true to himself: who, through the dissemblance, is consistent in the role.

Minor characters also highlight matters of sincerity and insincerity. The candour of Julie praying not according to 'les formules apprises' but 'selon la dictée de son cœur' (p.34), is a foil to the fraudulence of Anthime. After the formalities of Amédée's funeral, one glimpses Carola, placing her bunch of asters and crying in the rain: a moment of genuine emotion, wearing no public masks. Such glimmers are will o' the wisps, counterpointing pretence and making sincerity more elusive. The Marquis de Gesvres, who taught Lafcadio 'dressing up', is a blend of nature and artifice. In him, we learn, the two are not at odds: 'son élégance était parfaitement naturelle, comme une seconde sincérité' (p.88). Does this apply to Gide the author? Does he not attain a 'second sincerity' in artfulness, a greater truth through irony, disguise and stylistic costuming than through direct self-expression or identification with a single character, which are merely other forms of literary imposture? As Camus writes: 'Les auteurs de confession écrivent surtout pour ne pas se confesser ... Quand ils prétendent passer aux aveux, c'est le moment de se méfier'.[2] So, by being more devious ('par amour du détour'), the author of *Les Caves*, this book of 'bewares', is arguably being more honest.

So to the question of truth and falsity in art. For nowhere are representation and misrepresentation more sharply debated. And nowhere are the themes of reality and illusion, *vrai* and *vraisemblable*, sincerity and trust more strenuously tested than in the form and techniques of the fictional work itself. The novel is a place of 'make believe': an exercise in the art of seeming true more extensive than that worked on the credulous by Protos. Julius, by his father's biography, shows the slippery relations of life and art, and the problems of mimesis: 'il n'avait donné dans *L'Air des cimes* qu'une image édulcorée de sa vie, et réduite à l'insignifiance'

---

[2] *La Chute*, Gallimard, 1956, pp.140-41.

(p.67). It is Julius, too, who confuses the claims of the real and the fictional, saying, 'Les joies que je goûte en écrivant sont supérieures à celles que je pourrais trouver à vivre' (p.79); and who, reading of Amédée's death, cannot keep literature and life in their 'compartments' (see p.207). Lafcadio cannot easily correlate fact and fiction: 'Qu'il y a loin, entre l'imagination et le fait!' (p.195), words also hinting at the distances involved in the transformation of life into art, impossible to retrace. Where, indeed, does Gide's text lie between imagination and fact? The author invokes the convention that 'all is true': 'Mais il est de fait *historique* que, vers la fin de l'année 1893, le bruit en courut' (p.96). He introduces a footnote as 'extra-textual' evidence, quoting bibliographical details, publisher's address and date, so situating events in the 'reality' of time and space. But is this not another *cachot*, a textual hidey-hole, the reader's equivalent of Amédée's quest to chase things to their verifiable origins? And in purporting to play the honest broker by revealing the identity of the false priest: 'J'avertis honnêtement le lecteur: c'est lui qui se présente aujourd'hui sous l'aspect et le nom emprunté du chanoine de Virmontal' (p.97), is not the narrator pulling a fast one in that he and Protos are mirrors, each trying to con his audience, to pass off falsity as truth with the aid of potted history, each dressed as someone else? The literary work is the true crookery: a place of double dealing and dishonest practice. (1893, used here to authenticate fiction as fact, was the date of Gide's North African journeys and the undermining of his first faith.)

'A qui se fier?' There is no greater practiser of duplicity than the author, acting through his fictional double or alias, the narrator. The narrator is both reflection of the author and travesty, a complex system of textual disguise. In the literary journey, is he a more faithful guide than Protos? Can one be sure of his role? For, in the game of what is known and not known, he is the leading actor. At one time he is incorruptible omniscient presence, correcting factual errors, not letting characters get away with minor deceptions, seeing into their minds to clarify what they cannot see for themselves: as when he exposes Anthime's falsehood, '"Depuis quinze jours", a-t-il dit: en vérité ses rats ne jeûnent que depuis quatre' (p.19) or probes Lafcadio's blind spots, 'Il ne prenait pas garde à ceci, ou ne savait pas encore que ...' (p.185). But at others he professes ignorance of their inner movements, as if they were a living enigma, and he their quizzical onlooker. So, when he says (sketching the image of another novelist!), 'je ne suis pas bien sûr que Julius [...] ne se fit pas un jeu de tourner autour du scandale' (p.233), or of Carola, 'Je ne sais trop que penser de Carola Venitequa' (p.143), he gives his characters a reality of flesh and blood beyond his ambit. And when he says of Beppo, 'Plus tard il volera peut-être; il tuera même ...' (p.33), he admits evolutionary possibilities and a psychological *disponibilité* not in his hands. Indeed, how far is the text out of the author's hands? For when he speaks of the problem of ordering material, saying, 'tant que je n'aurai pas plus sûrement appris à démêler l'accidentel du nécessaire' (p.16), he suggests that he, like Amédée, is in an exploratory dark, unable to distinguish significant from non-significant, and that the novel as held by the reader is not ruled by a finality but still evolving with a liberty of its own. So, Anthime's *libre pensée* and the author's are questioned in parallel. But is this a further hoax to make one believe that what is fixed is *disponible*, what is *fermé* is *ouvert*, and that the arch-manipulator and literary overseer is, in all innocence, in the same position as the reader, having exercised no *droit de retouche*?

There are endless examples of a mock-complicity with the reader, the better to deceive. Referring to amorous episodes in Julius's life, the narrator pretends to respect the character's reputation and our sensitivities by adding: 'je n'en parlerais ici, si ses premiers romans ne l'avaient clairement laissé entendre' (p.21), as if his utterances were '*author*ized' by the writings of his character, and he were a man of conservative good taste, not the provocative, *risqué* and sacrilegious novelist we know him to be in *Les Caves* (*caveat lector*!). In setting the record straight with the words, 'Je ne voudrais pas qu'on se méprît sur le caractère de Julius' (p.54), he is not only upholding his 'hero' the better to sell him, but passing himself off as guarantor of truth in a text built on misapprehensions. And when he says of Anthime's limping movements to the Madonna, 'Cette hâte infirme est tragique pour nous' (p.32), it is anything but tragic, the word itself being a charade, hollowed by stylistic 'over-kill' and the accompanying comic-strip humour.

At this level, too, can one trust words? It is hardly an accident that, within a few lines of the fastidious narrator presenting the false 'Chanoine de Virmontal' with the words 'si j'ose dire' (p.94), we find Protos tricking the Comtesse with identical words 'si j'ose dire': a perfect mirroring. So, when the 'friendly' narrator warns Lafcadio of pitfalls, saying, 'Lafcadio, mon ami, vous donnez dans un fait divers' (p.64) or 'Lafcadio, mon ami, vous donnez dans le plus banal' (p.75), the intervention is suspect. Not only is it a 'transgression' in that he leaves the third personal realm for the second, joining the characters on their plane; but it implies that events are beyond his control and he can only alert the hero who is a free agent: a fudging of boundaries which further fuels the literature-life debate. Moreover, what seems to be genuine solicitude, an emotional bond between author and 'favourite son', is a literary artifice, a trick of the pen. And, fearing that Lafcadio will lapse into banality and having said 'N'attendez pas que je rapporte les propos interrompus d'une foule, les cris' (p.64), Gide proceeds to do just that, indulging in unashamed melodrama, pathos and suspense: a show worthy of Baldi, the illusionist. 'Ma plume vous abandonne', threatened the narrator. Not so: the author-impostor enjoys the performance, and one wonders if his lofty 'principles' are more reliable than Anthime's, mere camouflage. Does he, then, cheat readers and characters alike? It is an ironical coincidence that, as Amédée says, 'Dieu me guidera jusqu'à Rome' (p.121), a different voice comes from on high, that of the authorial god, intervening to ensure the pilgrim's departure: 'Ah! par pitié, Madame, ne le retenez pas! Il est si peu d'êtres sur terre qui savent trouver leur emploi'. In view of subsequent events, this heart-felt cry on one's 'true calling' rings singularly hollow (more so than the divine voice which lures Anthime to his vocation of dispossession). And who shows the greater 'good faith': Amédée in his pious ignorance, or the supportive author giving his creature (like the rats) a helping hand towards a blind alley? If one were inclined to give the narrator the benefit of the doubt, on the unlikely grounds that he is not omniscient but, in the evolving fiction, as accident-prone as anyone else, this is clearly not the case when he exhorts Lafcadio to yield to his better nature and help an old man groping for his glasses: 'Allons! Lafcadio, un bon mouvement! Cède à ton cœur, qui n'est pas corrompu. Viens en aide à l'infirme' (p.219). For here he knows that the old man is Protos in disguise, so leading his 'friend' into error with malicious relish, heightened by the irony that he does so by appealing to generosity and purity of spirit. And this is the same literary guardian who, previously, sought to guide Lafcadio away from pitfalls: a Janus who befriends and betrays.

4. Consequence and Inconsequence

The author's reference to the *accidentel* and the *nécessaire* is crucial. It poses, on the literary plane, the question implicit in Anthime's attempt to construct a deterministic scientific world around him. Is a world ruled by necessity, with no stray parts, an imposture? So, the writer asks how, in his evolving text, he can know what is significant or non-significant, central or marginal, and order his version accordingly, putting things in a chain of cause and effect which might explain, justify and 'redeem' their wandering absurdity.

At the same point Gide advertises Anthime's 'loupe' – 'Ça lui était venu il ne savait comment' (p.16) – so foreshadowing the inexplicable arrival of the Virgin, the 'miracle' which defies causality. He also asks if the unsightly growth has affected his so-called *libre pensée*: a hint of the unclear interplay of liberty and determinism in human motivation. Anthime fears prayer as a stab in the dark which swops scientific certainty and the security of 'l'ordre naturel des effets et des causes' (p.28) for an unfathomable order which may be no order at all. His rats' 'manna from heaven', his vision and Lafcadio's windfall are all interventions from unknown sources. Similarly, though Amédée, encountering Baptistin, finds that 'par une conjoncture providentielle'(p.135) they are going the same way, what is fortuitous and what deliberate is unsure, and the 'conjoncture' is far from obvious. The pilgrim fails to see significances where they exist, looks for 'Providence' in the wrong place, and attributes causality to what has none. So, he sees a *necessary* correlation between his inflamed spot and having sinned. One invokes and justifies the other: 'la cause profonde, celle qui lui méritait ce châtiment...' (p.169). And though exiled from God, he can still clutch, in the idea of merit and reward, at a remnant of order beyond the contingent and the accidental.

The theme of links is omnipresent. The wandering cuff-link is but one manifestation. When Anthime sees the 'mince *chaînette* d'argent' of Julie's holy medallion, the detail (like the 'chaînons d'une gourmette' of Diderot's *Jacques le fataliste*) is specifically tied to the idea of purposes: 'ça n'est pas joli-joli, mais je pense que cela sert à quelque chose' (p.24) – words reinforced by Lafcadio's assertion that 'je n'ai jamais recherché que ce qui ne peut pas me servir' (pp.89-90): that which has no bond of necessity. The 'liens de parenté' of the book are equally problematical. Unlike Amédée who 'n'avait d'autre ambition que de succéder à son père' (p.112), Lafcadio knows no line of descendency or law of succession, and is happily disconnected. Unaware of family links, he asks of Amédée: 'Entre ce sale magot et moi, quoi de commun?' (p.189). And the 'missing link' between this wimp and Julius baffles him (see p.199). Relations between characters are subject to wrong connections: Julius assumes that it is via Carola that Lafcadio knows he is in Rome, whereas it is via Amédée, Lafcadio's link with Carola having been broken. Protos's story provokes a chain reaction. But it has, even for him, unexpected consequences: 'la prédication de Pau portait fruit; mais non point précisément la sorte de fruits qu'eût pu souhaiter Protos' (p.142). Fruit as unwelcome as the offshoot Julius has found on his family tree!

The text is a breeding-ground for all that upsets sequences and predictable progressions. Anthime's world of consequentiality and perfect equations, where 'dans les plus surprenants mouvements de l'être on pouvait uniment reconnaître une parfaite obéissance à l'agent' (p.13), is rocked by the insubordination of the miracle. Julius's logically stage-managed writings, where psychology grows perfectly from its mould, with no stray impulses or evolutionary hiccups, are challenged by Lafcadio, capricious and unpredictable, who scorns the 'ragoût de logique' on which Julius feeds character and the 'souci de le maintenir [...] conséquent avec vous et avec soi-même' (p.90): 'true to itself', arrested in a phoney time and space. The S.O.S. from Rome snaps Amédée's continuity. The journey is his 'acte gratuit': without preparation or forethought ('Tu n'as rien de prêt', p.121) and no clue how to proceed. An act without a past,

unheralded by what has preceded, and without a future, unable to
reach an intended goal. And, despite his neat timetable and wish for
a '*bénigne* aventure', a word which for him, as for Anthime (see
p.13), means without incident or anything un*toward*, life proves that
it defies convenient symmetry and is, like Amédée himself,
abundantly accident-prone.

Lafcadio is the champion of discontinuity. He burns his
mementos, casts off Carola as a deterministic relic of former
relationships, and makes a clean sweep of his life: 'occupons-nous à
liquider notre passé' (p.73). He disproves the law which says that
one must be one's own sequel. Defouqueblize also stresses how 'un
trou dans la mémoire [...] une simple interruption de courant'
(p.226) can unhitch one from a false persona. Lafcadio urges the
'professor' to enjoy his own 'break' from academic behaviour,
saying, 'En voyage [...] cela ne tire pas à conséquence' (p.224). If,
as for Amédée, a journey is 'la cessation d'une continuité', then
what one does on it is, arguably, a matter of no consequence. Julius
and Lafcadio have already debated the issue, the lad claiming to be
'un être d'inconséquence' (p.90), to which the rationalist retorts,
'Persuadez-vous d'abord qu'il n'y a pas d'inconséquence, non plus
en psychologie qu'en physique': a debate pursued, not only in the
characters' evolutions, but in the literary act itself, balanced as it is
between premeditation and the accidents of words, determinism of
development and a constantly sprouting textual *disponibilité*.

The text frustrates attempts to move in straight lines. The
detour is its hallmark. Anthime the 'faux dieu' bars Véronique from
'paradise', closing the direct route to the garden and forcing her to
go the long way round. Is this so different from Amédée's fall from
grace and long-winded journey, where, instead of proceeding to his
destination, he misses a connection, takes a side-line to Arles and
'dut redéfaire la route' (p.128)? Protos describes the bastard as
being 'le produit d'une incartade, d'un crochet dans la droite ligne'
(p.226): the product of an irregularity on the side, a deviant side-
shoot in the linear genealogy of the family tree. Lafcadio himself,
bound for Julius's house, does from personal whim and love of
lateral thinking what Véronique had to do by necessity, take the

roundabout route: 'Par amour du détour [...] Lafcadio prenait par le plus long' (p.75) – on which detour Geneviève overtakes him and vanishes round a turning (ibid.). Later he has the urge to '*détourner* Geneviève de son père' (p.248, my emphasis): to tempt her from the straight and narrow. Even when in Rome, the justification of his travels, something deflects Amédée from the obvious direction (p.135). The route to his hotel follows a succession of foreign streets, via Viminale, via Agostino Depretis, via Nazionale, until he loses grip of his starting-point and the journey collapses into namelessness: 'à partir de quoi ils progressèrent à travers un labyrinthe de ruelles sans nom' (p.136). Even the stairway defeats efforts to get there in one go: 'l'escalier hésitant, biaisant, s'y reprenant à trois fois avant de parvenir à l'étage' (p.137). Protos leads Amédée all round the houses, literally and figuratively. When the simpleton wants to go straight to Cardinal San-Felice, the criminal (who raises the question of 'going straight' in another sense) exclaims: 'Quoi! votre intention pouvait-elle être de l'aller trouver tout de go? [...] et de vous ouvrir à lui *sans detour!* (p.149, my emphasis). This phrase echoes, via its own 'corridors souterrains', throughout the text. Lafcadio dismisses Julius's book as 'sans détour ni mystère' (p.62); Fleurissoire and Blafaphas, mooning over Arnica, become story-tellers like Julius, narrative expressions of one-track minds and unilinear lives, 'se racontaient [...] sans détours, les moindres mots...' (p.113); and Defouqueblize says ironically (for he is deviousness itself), 'croyez-vous que je l'oserais exprimer sans plus de détours, si seulement nous étions à Bordeaux?' (p.224), implying that it is only now that he is off the leash that he can afford straight speaking. (Directness or indirectness of language is central to the *sotie*.) Even Julius diverts Amédée. Far from restoring the connection with home, his fractured, inconsequential speech tips things further into the centrifugal. Their minds take different tracks; neither can keep to the point; one man's *conséquence* is another's *inconséquence*. First one, then the other draws his opposite number physically into a side-street, off the beaten track (see pp.174, 177). And each voices a reminder that they are straying from the subject: 'pardonnez-moi: je

m'écartais de ma visite' (p.175) and 'Je crains, dit doucement
Amédée, que vous ne vous écartiez de nouveau' (p.176).

The novel is a multiplication of routes. 'Ce vieillard est un
carrefour' (p.201), says Lafcadio of Amédée. 'Je suis à un tournant
de ma vie' (p.203), exclaims Julius. Even the Madonna, who moves
in mysterious ways, is the 'Madone tri*via*le' (p.30, my emphasis),
Madonna of the three ways or, in translation for less (or more)
subtils a few pages later, 'la statue du *carrefour*' (p.36, my
emphasis). Protos's network, with its 'ramifications ténébreuses'
(p.141), is 'le Mille-Pattes': an image of other things with branches
everywhere, like the family tree, and the text. Characters meet and
part. Protos tells Amédée that, though on the same route, they
should, for safety's sake, split up: 'quand nous approcherons de sa
villa, nous nous séparerons s'il vous plaît. Vous me suivrez de loin'
(p.155). Julius, too, barely reunited with Amédée, suggests a parting
of the ways: 'Allons; il faut nous séparer' (p.184), words marking
the end of Part Four and a switch to a new character on a new line.
People have the same destination but different routes. Amédée and
Julius head Popewards, but for diverse reasons. Julius and Lafcadio
set off simultaneously for the 'father', but one arrives first, a fact
which would have mortified Julius 's'il avait pu savoir qui venait de
le *devancer* près du vieux' (p.74, my emphasis) – a rhyme for
Protos's 'Vous me suivrez de loin', as if to show that a *subtil* will be
always one move ahead. It anticipates the scene where Lafcadio and
Julius chase each other at different speeds on parallel tracks,
without ever coinciding: 'Ainsi tour à tour bondissant et dépassant,
puis dépassé, on eût dit que l'un jouait à saute-mouton avec l'autre'
(p.206).

The book's disruptive mobility depends on the to-ings and fro-
ings of trains. Lafcadio, like Amédée, finds that the train has set off
(to Naples) before he realizes; he takes the first train back to Rome
next day – another leg of a journey written off. And in the
penultimate chapter, Anthime and wife, coming from Milan third
class, are on the same train as Marguerite and daughter, coming
from Paris in the sleeper, all bound for Rome (but in the other
direction from Lafcadio), having boarded at different points of the

trajet and knowing nothing of each other's presence there: a variation on the idea of following at a distance. The police, pursuing their 'recherches le long de la voie' (pp.201, 208) in straight lines of enquiry, fail to take account of the many ramifications, sidetracks and backtracks, and come to the wrong conclusions. All roads lead to Rome, but in patterns so complex that the eternal city loses its value as stable centre of a clearly ordered universe. Significantly, Anthime's property holdings in Egypt have changed value beyond all expectation because of the 'nouvelle ligne de chemin de fer du Caire à Héliopolis' (p.27): a further example of fortunes altered by the unpredictabilities of a railway line, and of a city (City of the Sun, supposed centre of the universe) ultimately connected with dispossession, upheaval and disorientation. *Les Caves du Vatican* is a forerunner to Butor's *La Modification*, where the journey to Rome and the textual journey become a plurality of structural lines, in an experience which is not an arrival and a closure but the opening of multi-directional *fissures*, causing the traveller to requestion his relationship with reality and the very nature of reality itself.

Gide's text is an antidote to the determinism of the Naturalist novel and its pseudo-scientific supports. Hence the ironic reference to the 'impasse Claude Bernard' (suggesting a dead-end in literary research and the need for more spacious avenues). Its plot is a network of unpredictabilities. Things come out of the blue or take unforeseen turns. Characters bump into each other, sometimes literally, as when Julius meets Carola or Lafcadio and Geneviève collide on the stairs. There are blind corners and dog-legs (see p.53); and as Defouqueblize reaches the 'dernier coude du couloir' (p.218), he is jolted sideways, 'unsighted' in two senses, into a reunion with Lafcadio. The verb 'croiser' recurs (cf. p.188). The book is a mesh of coincidences, tangents and intersections, forming an immeasurable *carrefour*.

The essential links of structure may not therefore be found in the broad lines of narrative progression but in less obvious connections. One might not notice, since it straddles two languages, the five parts of the book, and two characters (Anthime and Lafcadio) antithetically apart, that the opening topic of *guérison* recurs in the Conrad quotation heading the Fifth Part: 'the question is not how to get cured' (p.185). Situations recur, almost identically – the 'apparitions' of the Virgin and the sylph-like Geneviève, Lafcadio bowed solemnly before his father and Julius before the Holy Father, Lafcadio counting to twelve before addressing Juste-Agénor and before throwing Amédée from the train – so teasing a 'séquence subtile et cachée' from apparent 'inconséquence', and testing the reader's abilities as traveller. They are also a test of one's literary memory, a structural challenge to be a *subtil*, giving a new slant to Protos's comments on 'un trou dans la mémoire [...] la cessation d'une continuité' (p.226). A peripheral mention may acquire unexpected significance at a new juncture. An allusion on page 32 to the religious statue not being the modern sort made of 'carton-romain plastique de Blafaphas, la maison d'art Fleurissoire-Lévichon' seems a throw-away comment. But it is the germ of an account in Part Three of the fortunes of the name Fleurissoire, and of a footnote on page 114 (a mere side-line of the text) quoting from the brochure for *Carton-Romain-Plastique* which, it says, 'remplace fort avantageusement le carton-pierre, le papier-stuc [...] dont l'usage n'a que trop bien établi toute la défectuosité'. Is this a dig at how easily the Madonna's hand broke off? In which case it contradicts the narrator's earlier praise of her old-style manufacture, so subjecting the detail to divergences of valuation. Be that as it may, this is a prime example of uncertainty as to what, in the patterning, is *accidentel* or *nécessaire*, marginal or central, *inconséquent* or *conséquent*, even if such consequence emerges eighty pages later, with few traces of continuity. A *subtil* may even detect that the writer, in describing *Carton-Romain-Plastique*, mirrors his own technique in his use of this detail: 'Cette invention, qui d'abord n'avait l'air de rien ...' (p.114).

Gide delights in interruption. Not only do characters say, 'Séparons-nous'. The author, too, as if some reason wills that they should no longer be seen together, leaves his characters and takes a different track. So, Anthime's life-story is suspended, not to be resumed until Part Five, by which time our journey is twistier than Amédée's. At the end of Part Two, we leave Lafcadio as he departs:

'*It is time to launch the ship*' (p.91), joint victims of the lack of forwarding address. We rejoin him after a break, an 'interruption de courant', knowing nothing of the interim or what brings him from Paris to Rome. And at the end of the book, one is left on the verge of possibilities: the text not as terminus but as *carrefour*, available for undetermined sequels.

Interruptions affect dialogue and communications. Trying to order his thoughts, Julius shows irritation with Fleurissoire: 'Mon cher Amédée, si vous m'interrompez tout le temps' (p.176). There is a hiatus, as a commissionaire brings in an envelope for Amédée – again to Julius's annoyance: 'Celui qui l'écrivit aurait du moins pu s'excuser de nous interrompre' (p.182). But this is not the only unapologetic writer in the vicinity. For when the narrator says elsewhere, 'N'attendez pas que je rapporte les propos *interrompus* d'une foule, les cris...' (p.64, my emphasis), ostensibly upholding an art which is *not* one of loose ends and incoherences, he is in fact practising an interruption of his own and causing a diversion. The reader's route to his destination does not run smooth. It is littered with author's 'asides', digressions and parentheses. It may be a mere confidence exchanged about Julius's character. Or a fuller interlude on the name Blafaphas, a mini-lecture then marginalized as if dispensable: 'Mais ces remarques philologiques ne sauraient intéresser qu'une classe assez restreinte de lecteurs' (p.111). Or the narrator himself may be caught in mid-flow by events, as when he is lyricizing over the 'widow' and the prospects dawning for Lafcadio: 'Ah! devant de tels êtres le démon céderait; pour de tels êtres, Lafcadio, ton cœur se dévouerait sans doute ... /A ce moment le garçon passa changer les assiettes' (p.222) – another linguistic excursion leading nowhere. In a book where a vital letter from Arnica to Amédée has scrawled across its fourth page an inconsequential jotting from Blafaphas asking him to find out, while in Italy, 'comment ils font le trou dans le macaroni' (p.172), one is justified in asking if the author is as committed as he says to 'ne relater que l'essentiel' (p.16). And when Protos insists that in Amédée's letter to the Cardinal 'rien de significatif ne fût dit' (p.151), or when Amédée advises Julius, 'Ayons l'air de parler de matières indifférentes' (p.177), one wonders where the lines are drawn linguistically between the significant and the non-significant, 'l'accidentel' and 'le nécessaire'.

5. The 'acte gratuit'

The textual climate breeds gratuitous events: events with no apparent justification for being, sparked by accident or chance. And though the notion of an unconnected act is crystallized in Lafcadio's 'dispensing with' a complete stranger, it grows from a ground rich with trace elements and lengthily prepared. So, one wonders what qualifies as *acte gratuit* on this route of unpredictabilities. More significantly, Lafcadio's act comes as the supreme complex equation, both of his own psychological lines of force, and all the references, direct and indirect, to gratuity throughout the text, so that, ironically, its emergence seems endowed with a deep-rooted logical necessity.

The causality of good and evil, investment and return, is an early theme. Anthime gives his finances to the Church but to no avail, and the pact which says that goodness is rewarded or 'seek and ye shall find' breaks down. As with Amédée, faith is expended towards its own wastage. In reminding Julius, 'Tu m'as souvent dit que tu ne travaillais pas en vue de la récompense' (p.47), Marguerite also rehearses the theme of doing things for nothing, with no thought for consequences. Lafcadio, having saved the child, gives away the reward (pp.65-66), so freeing his act from any utilitarian motive which might jeopardize its integrity. Julius misreads entries in Lafcadio's diary referring to *punta*: 'Julius [...] prit "punta" pour une pièce de monnaie étrangère et ne vit dans ces comptes qu'un puéril et mesquin marchandage de mérites et de rétributions' (p.56) – just as Amédée sees his lapses within an order of 'mérites et rétribution' (see pp.166, 169). But Lafcadio shuns the money-principle. And, while Protos amasses thousands by his dirty 'marchandage', Lafcadio defies the determinism, cornerstone of Balzacian fiction, which links psychology and gain.

Much attention focuses on keeping accounts. Lafcadio's

carnet has been given 'pour qu'il y inscrive ses comptes' (p.54). Amédée, on every leg of the journey, 'fit ses comptes et ses prières' (p.132): financial and spiritual needs in harness, linked to the same issue of what, in life, one can bargain for. Lafcadio, by contrast, abhors petty calculation as the enemy of the grand impulse. For, while the two cohabit, the true principle of the journey – to set off with no end in view, like those 'qui partent pour partir' – is compromised. *Les Caves* is, in many ways, an anti-economic work (not least in that its own journey, losing sight of points of departure and necessary arrivals, becomes an end in itself). Lafcadio symptomatically leaves the dead man's money: a gap of motivation which foils the efforts of investigators to 'integrate' the *acte gratuit*.

'Désintéressement', as opposed to the vested interest, is a major strand. Drafting a reply to his father's letter, Julius defends his intentions: 'rejetant le haut du corps en arrière, il demeura quelques instants, balançant sa phrase, la plume levée: *Il m'est dur de voir suspecter précisément par vous un désintéressement qui...* (p.48). But his denial of ulterior motive fits ill with the posturing and studied stylistic effects. To act without forethought, to give without counting the cost – 'dépenser [...] sans m'inquiéter par avance' (p.88) – is part of Lafcadio's code, as is his refusal of 'le besoin' and the boredom of the necessary. His attitude to his allowances (see p.89) is revealing: he opts not to know their origin, so to avoid indebtedness. And, after Amédée's murder, 'il se désintéressait des suites de son aventure' (p.217), as if not bound by the repercussions of its aftermath. 'Désintéressement' can also mean the clearing of debts or *owing nothing to anyone*: an apt description of how Lafcadio sees himself, and of the theoretical nature of the *acte gratuit*.

Disponibilité is the psychological correlative of the act. When Lafcadio comes into money, Julius says that it is lucky, for otherwise 'vous étiez prêt à tout'. 'Prêt à rien, au contraire' (p.89) is the reply. Lafcadio is, in a sense, ready for everything and ready for nothing, indefinitely available. His mental engagement-book is always free. He postpones reading of the death, preferring virtuality to the *fait accompli* (see p.200). The *acte gratuit* is also in a superior parenthesis. Like Lafcadio, it avoids ties and leaves no address.

To arouse doubt as to why things are there is not exclusive to the act. Protos fulfils the same role: 'je n'ai jamais compris ce qu'il faisait là' (p.87). And Amédée's God-centred universe where each part has purpose (like a mosquito's buzz, God's surety that *nothing comes without forewarning!*) yields to the thought that people are there for no penetrable reason – 'combien la présence des gens dans la rue est rarement justifiable' (p.154) – like the act which will mow him down.

The *acte gratuit* itself, which ought to occur without a word of warning, has a fictional trial run, before one even knows that Lafcadio will reappear. The seed which has germinated in Julius's mind, while off-stage, is the idea of an 'être d'inconséquence'. So, exit the safe biographical hero and enter the prototype for an unpredictable *nouveau roman*. The writer may fail to go the whole hog. For, just as he once insisted that 'il n'y a pas d'inconséquence' (p.90), he still holds that 'sans doute cette apparente inconséquence cache-t-elle une séquence plus subtile et cachée' (p.175); and while acknowledging the excessive logic of his previous characters, he is still conscious of 'leur insuffisante détermination' (ibid.), their need to be worked into yet more 'subtle' networks of psychological determinism. He also denies that sudden revelations (like Anthime's conversion or his own volte-face) spring from nowhere, but have a long incubation: 'on croirait à une illumination soudaine: au fond on n'arrêtait pas d'y penser' (ibid.). He has, however, gone far enough into the subversive idea to ditch the literary persona who was 'sans détour ni mystère', to admit hidden patterns of motivation, and to pen a portrait identical to the one Lafcadio will shortly assume. Not only does he foresee a character impervious to the usual profit-motive, but defines before its time the essence, the *raison d'être* one might say, of the *acte gratuit*. Pointing out the restrictive nature of traditions of thought stemming from La Rochefoucauld, which see human action as attributable to *amour-propre* or self-interest, he moots the possibility of totally disinterested actions. By this, he does not mean altruistic or charitable deeds performed against the baser impulses of human nature. On the contrary,

> Par *désintéressé*, j'entends: gratuit. Et que le mal, ce
> que l'on appelle: le mal, peut être aussi gratuit que le
> bien.
> – Mais, dans ce cas, pourquoi le faire?
> – Précisément! par luxe, par besoin de dépense, par jeu.
> (p.179)

Good and evil can be as 'meaningless' as each other: not done for this or that reason, or having opposite roles in a dualistic scheme of values, but committed – beyond morality or personal gain – for the mere pleasure of doing that for which there is no need. Good and evil (like truth and falsity in the book) thus lose their individual (or joint) *raison d'être*, and blur definitions. Julius also refers to keeping accounts, saying that, whereas 'à ce point de vue catholique, l'âme la mieux dressée est celle qui tient le mieux ses comptes' (pp.179-80) – the one who keeps a tidy book and stays in balance in the profit and loss account of good and evil, one can imagine a superior spirit, 'une âme qui ne tienne plus de comptes du tout', whose actions stem, not from what one will reap from them or where they figure in some kind of reckoning, but from spontaneity of doing with no end in mind. Hence his statement, spoken with surprising conviction: 'le mépris de ce qui peut servir [...] est signe d'une certaine aristocratie de l'âme'. But the crux of his thinking, which makes it the advance replica of Lafcadio's, is that if an act is *gratuit*, with no purposeful intent, then it cannot be traced to the perpetrator, for the law, working back from act to cause, relies on the logic of motive and profit: '*Is fecit cui prodest*' (p.182). Ironically, this heretical brain-wave comes to Julius in the Vatican in a moment's *distraction* (when his mind went off the track); and he calls it a revelation (hardly divine in its impious prospects, though giving the omniscience to foresee one episode of the future in its finest detail).

Gide has meticulously juxtaposed these two versions of the *acte gratuit*. Their distant interplay enriches the theme: 'Qu'il y a loin, entre l'imagination et le fait!' (p.195). Where one protagonist theorizes, the other acts. Where one gathers material for a fiction, the other performs in real life. (Seen at a further remove, of course, they are different degrees of fiction within Gide's text: one who acts within the fiction, one who fictionalizes within it.) In the structural patterning, they represent two tracks towards the same destination (with one traveller doomed to lag behind and suspend his journey at a safer earlier station). They illustrate, not so much a sequential progression as an obscure *simultanéisme*: common reverberations occurring simultaneously on separate wavelengths. Is this, as with the *acte gratuit*, pure chance or the product of a covert determinism? For Lafcadio's act, ostensibly detached from causal relationships, gains a precedent in Julius's scale model, so that one can 'see it coming' or at least see *conséquence* and continuity in it when it does come. Nor can one say who, on the trip, gets there first ('tour à tour bondissant et dépassant, puis dépassé'). For though Julius's thoughts have grown verbatim out of Lafcadio's statements, Lafcadio's thoughts on the train echo the Julius of Part Four, making one wonder who is derivative of whom. And though his version comes first as a hollow anticipation of the real thing, it is perhaps Julius who has the last word. Does not the novelist, in the end, always come out on top?

It is not difficult to find motives for Lafcadio's 'motiveless' act. Before the event, he is in an exceptional mental state. Is he undergoing his own crisis of identity, those doubts 'sur la réalité de sa pensée, sur l'authenticité de sa vie' which have unhinged Julius and Amédée in turn? There are things he prefers not to acknowledge, like the allowance which makes him a 'kept man'. He is sensitive to the need to stay true to himself, despite changed circumstances (see p.185). But the eagle-eyed narrator sees him already on the slippery slope of self-betrayal: 'Il ne prenait pas garde à ceci, ou ne savait pas encore que, pour lui, désormais, le goût des mets allait changer'. The balance between *nécessité* and *jeu* is upset: '...maintenant que ne le pressait plus le besoin, sa résistance se relâchait' (ibid.). His life, too, is at a crossroads and he would take any direction, Java or wherever, to relieve his dissatisfactions. The past has caught up with him: in the debts left by his 'uncle' (an image of freedom turned into a liability), and as parentage and financial patronage. Whatever his nostalgias, he must swallow the pill: 'je suis Baraglioul' (p.186).

The detail of the old Italian woman whose bag he carried during the carefree travels of youth is revealing. It is part of a series of disconnected musings as the train carries him along. He remembers this as a 'good deed' in the Christian sense. Does some perverse instinct now prompt him to reverse it and prove himself beyond moral determinism, bestriding good and evil indifferently like a colossus? Lafcadio gave the old lady a kiss but, he confesses, 'je l'aurais tout aussi bien serrée à la gorge [...] quand j'ai senti cette sale peau ridée sous mon doigt ... Ah! comme elle caressait le col de ma veste [...] en disant: *figlio mio! carino!*' (pp.186-87). Is the horror of being claimed as someone's son and smothered with affection so acute that it feeds an unprecedented act of revolt? As Amédée enters, he makes sheep's eyes at the winsome lad, saying to himself in words which are a translation of the Italian woman's *carino*, 'Ah! l'aimable garçon!' (p.189). And quite irrationally, Lafcadio is revulsed by the idea that one might kiss such a lamentable specimen: 'Qu'a-t-il à me sourire ainsi? Pense-t-il que je vais l'embrasser! Se peut-il qu'il y ait des femmes pour caresser encore les vieillards!' (ibid.). Not only does the verb 'caresser' link directly with the old woman's actions, but Amédée, too, is soon preoccupied with his 'col' and 'veste' (p.193). Nor is his skin in A1 condition! All of which facilitates a slippage between the two 'stories', and an unwitting substitution of *personnages*. (Is the mental switching of an 'étrange vieillard' for a 'vieille' so preposterous in an atmosphere where Protos tells Amédée to call the false Cardinal San-Felice '*Ma vieille*' (p.151), and Amédée confuses masculine and feminine by using *Grazia* to a lady?) Amédée's apparition may be seen, then, as a heaven-sent opportunity for Lafcadio to 'settle accounts', while reaffirming himself as 'être d'inconséquence'. The urge to go against the grain of conventional morality is indicated by a reference, again disconnected from anything we know of his history, to the 'curé de Covigliajo': a religious figure whose endearments he resented and tried unsuccessfully to alienate. Is the *acte gratuit* therefore a religious exorcism, an attempt to get his own back, like Anthime's iconoclastic act, on a residual figure or symbolic value lurking in his conscience? Is it, in a deeper sense, a paying off of debts? Lafcadio despises his own charms and wants to prove the world wrong by belying appearances and becoming an object of repugnance. Carola has suggested eating garlic or blackening his face. Lafcadio now seems very tempted by the idea, figuratively speaking, of 'blackening his face': a link of rare finesse, since Amédée has chosen this compartment because of the 'air sombre' of an Italian in a previous one and the 'regard candide' of the 'aimable garçon' in this.

That the recollection centres on an old woman, and poses the question of life or death, is significant. For there is evidence that Lafcadio is haunted by premature age. He recalls a young lad in the charge of the 'curé de Covigliajo' whom he would have loved as a companion, saying, 'Quels beaux yeux il levait vers moi! qui cherchaient aussi inquiètement mon regard que mon regard cherchait le sien' (p.188) – a reciprocity which makes Amédée's oglings, unanswered by Lafcadio's 'œil morne', grotesque. 'Qu'est-ce que j'étais à cet âge?', he goes on, 'Un *stripling* plein de convoitise, que j'aimerais rencontrer aujourd'hui' (ibid.). Not only does this show a craving for youth and a rift in the self, but prepares for an alternative encounter widening the divorce between real and ideal. And when Amédée comes through the sliding-door, prompting the words 'D'où sort cet étrange vieillard?' (p.189), it could be an image from Lafcadio's subconscious, so easily does it slip from the meanderings of rêverie, or a disenchanted question addressed to himself. The 'apparition' is a threatening icon, to be suppressed. In this sense, too, there is not far between 'l'imagination et le fait'. And the question 'd'où sort?', applying to origins, family roots and root causes, is relevant to the springs of the subconsciousness and to the *acte gratuit*. What irony that the sombre occupant of the previous compartment was 'un Italien *entre deux âges*' (ibid., my emphasis). For, in changing carriages, Amédée has gone from the frying pan into the fire, little knowing how explosive the gap between two ages can be!

Lafcadio longs for former playmates. In succession (pp.186-88) he yearns for the Marquis de Gesvres, Julius and Protos, in each case using the tense of wishful thinking or 'would have beens'. Hence, his dozing recollection of an enchanted moment with 'uncle' Wladi, the person most able to turn one's 'existence un peu rassise' into a 'fête éperdue' (p.84). The escapade was a midnight prowl about the house, where all seemed larger than life, charged with suspense – a celebration of the 'appétit d'amusement' (p.191), regardless of where it led or whether one believed in it or not. And the final act, a furtive sip of wine, was less important than the pleasure of leaving no tell-tale signs, and going back to sleep where one left off: 'Ni vu, ni connu' (p.192). Is there not again a mental overspill between the two 'journeys', with Lafcadio between fiction and reality, subject to alternations and 'interruptions de courant'? Is his starved spirit of play seeking to reassert itself *à la Wladi*, with him now as *metteur en scène* in organizing someone's journey of surprises in the night, and no-one to find him out: a game of follow-my-leader, spread across time, which even the original guide and mentor could not have foreseen? For Cadio says of his charismatic 'role model': 'il est si prodigieusement amusé par Wladi qu'il traverserait du feu pour le suivre' (p.191). Perhaps he is doing just that: following him but at such a distance (like Amédée behind Protos) that no-one will see the connection. For, just as he says in *his* narration 'Wladi redonne un peu de lumière' (p.192), so *our* narrator says of him 'Lafcadio redonna de la lumière' (p.194): replicas of each other, adjusting their stage lighting as one, except that Lafcadio's theatre has no worthwhile players.

There is also a feeling that 'the end is nigh': of a world in decline heading for an apocalyptic finale. Though commenting on Julius as an anachronism in a society which no longer reads, Lafcadio's diagnosis may reflect a similar feeling of *his* redundancy in an unappreciative world: 'Ça finira par une catastrophe; quelque belle catastrophe, tout imprégnée d'horreur! on foutra l'imprimé par-dessus bord; et ce sera miracle si le meilleur ne rejoint pas au fond le pire' (p.187). Why else should he need to prove himself to the ignoramus opposite, saying, 'Il serait bien surpris sans doute d'apprendre que je sais lire écriture ou imprimé, couramment, à l'envers ou par transparence' (p.189)? Is he so desperate for an audience? The word 'imprimé' recurs, suggesting a transference between the two contexts; and the idea of throwing something overboard is ominously latent. The anticipation of a fateful coming together of *le meilleur* and *le pire* links with kissing or throttling the old woman; and after saving a life, it is only a swing of the pendulum to take one with equanimity. The premonition of 'quelque belle catastrophe' is a projection of his private sense of an end of an era, and the seemingly objective justification of its further recklessness. It feeds indifference, in the sense of life and death becoming equals: 'Je me sentais d'étreinte assez large pour embrasser l'entière humanité; ou l'étrangler peut-être' (p.187) – a kind of Baudelairean *ennui* which 'dans un bâillement avalerait le monde'. It favours a detachment from human vanity which makes others' lives and his own worthless pawns: 'Que peu de chose la vie humaine! Et que je risquerais la mienne agilement, si seulement s'offrait quelque belle prouesse un peu joliment téméraire à oser!' (ibid.). Lafcadio, then, seeks some extravagant exploit, a final fling, and looks outside for opportunities, as if it were to blame for his barrenness. Lafcadio has always been curious to provoke the unprecedented and see what he is capable of. But the resurgence of the appetite to know *'ce qui arriverait si'* (ibid.), which he admits is 'ce qui me porte à agir' (in other words, his *motivating* force), is fuelled now by the thought that 'Dieu est mort' (if He ever existed) and that 'tout est permis'. And in saying '"Que tout ce qui peut être soit!" c'est comme ça que je m'explique la Création' (ibid.), he is proposing a highly 'chancy' view of Providence in which the Creator, craving surprises like himself, launched an exploratory act with no special reason for being but simply to see what might happen. (This is not the only time that the book suggests human life itself as the fundamental *acte gratuit*.) He is thus a *surhomme*,

enjoying that 'vaniteux plaisir de faux dieu' which gave Anthime
power of life and death over insignificant creatures. His contempt
for the human puppet-show, voiced in his 'Belle collection de
marionnettes ... ' (p.188), sparks the need to disrupt the drab
repertoire and jerk some outrageous response. Hence the question,
'Cadio, mon petit, le problème se pose: faire accroc à cette destinée.
Mais par où?' (p.190): how to hijack this life-form and its
predictable ways. The role of perverse puppeteer is inseparable from
saying farewell to the world: 'Allons! plions bagage; il est temps!
En fuite vers un nouveau monde' (p.188). That there will be no
connection with his new life (in the Borneo jungle or wherever)
frees him to bring down the curtain and make his exit with a
stunning *deus ex machina*, a visiting-card which no-one will be able
to follow up: 'Ni vu, ni connu [...] Qui le saurait?' (pp.192-94). He
will relish, *in absentia*, the confusion of the police (p.194) – as well
as his cleverness, in this rare test for which he would surely award
himself 'douze points' in his account-book of *punte*.

   One could delve *ad infinitum* into the motivations of the
'crime immotivé': how Amédée's irritating switching on and off of
the lights may have prompted Lafcadio to snuff *his* light once and
for all; how the lad's pique that Amédée shows no inclination to
open his case, so frustrating his own little *roman policier*, may have
triggered the urge to open *his* 'case' or box and send him flying
from the compartment; and so on. The *acte gratuit* is a kind of *mise
en abyme*, into which one is sucked speculatively as if into a
psychological abyss. It is also a kind of fraud: unlike Protos's hoax
played on others, a deception by Lafcadio on himself. Prior to the
event, several references to honesty well up. We learn how averse
our hero is to swindling and double dealing: 'Lafcadio répugnait
aux filouteries' (p.185). He queries his own authenticity: 'Est-ce le
fait d'un honnête homme, Lafcadio ...' And of Faby's lack of
openness about his homosexual leanings, he says: 'Mais combien sa
retenue m'agaçait!' (p.188), as if he, by contrast, is now holding
back nothing. Yet the *acte gratuit* is fraught with contradictions:
inevitably, perhaps, when it enlists so many subconscious selves.
And just as a whiff of dishonesty rose from his burning photos, now

there are veils of dubious thinking and disguise. He censors reality, retreats under his hat, grudgingly opens half an eye, forces himself to doze off and conjure the images he wants to see. He is play-acting to himself, imagining what impression he would make on his 'implied reader': 'Drôle de jeu pour un enfant! Qu'eût pensé de cela Julius?' (p.192). By a process of substitution, he ascribes to others what stems only from himself: he blames Amédée for failing to satisfy *his* expectations, *his* sense of excitement, or to become the obliging character of *his* fictions (the very aberration for which he derided Julius). He convinces himself that to do away with this weed would be a charitable act, not caring to see that 'the fault lies in ourselves'. Is he, then, cheating at his own game? He uses 'purely' numerical chance to say if Amédée should be flung from the train, as if something else ultimately determined the issue. But as he counts to twelve – 'Une; deux; trois; quatre; (lentement! lentement!) cinq; six; sept; huit; neuf ... Dix, un feu ...' (p.195) – he 'doctors' the result, no doubt according to sneaking preferences, by slowing down or suspending the count: another sequence not allowed to proceed to its destination. And the mental time taken by the wilful words 'lentement! lentement!' is that between ten and twelve, a man's life or death. When throwing a dice to decide whether to leave the train, he gets out regardless of not having thrown a six: so disclaiming preferences while exercising them, giving up 'ownership' while reserving all the rights. Is this different from accepting money but choosing not to know where it comes from? Or from bending the meanings of words when he reads the newspaper report of his 'crime' (see p.200)? Indeed, for a man ostensibly dissociated from personal choice, Lafcadio remains peculiarly 'choosy'. And for one who has allowed the *acte gratuit* its freedom, divorced from intentions of his own, it may seem inconsistent to say, 'Allons, allons; Cadio, pas de retouches: tout est comme tu l'as voulu' (p.196), as if it does, after all, depend on pre-existent designs. It is left to the unlikely Julius to pin-point the contradictions. In a duet oscillating between real and unreal as did Lafcadio's encounter with Amédée, the Count notes that the perpetrator of such a crime is 'à l'abri du besoin [...] Mais ces seules

occasions le tentent qui exigent de lui quelque habileté' (p.206): free
from necessity but drawn irresistibly by certain kinds of exploits. He
is 'un homme libre', but 'à la merci de la première occasion'
(p.207): perhaps as much a victim of Anthime's *tropismes*, however
subtle the stimuli, or one of the 'collection de marionnettes',
however complex the strings. 'Puis l'impunité l'encourage ... Mais
elle le dépite à la fois', adds Julius, showing a man in a vicious
circle, wanting to get off but contemptuous of easy victories and
trying all the harder to be caught. And though motives galore may
elude him, he nails Lafcadio in the fundamental paradox when he
says: 'Sa raison de commettre le crime, c'est précisément de le
commettre sans raison'.

The *acte gratuit* becomes a conglomeration of ironies, mostly
at Lafcadio's expense. 'Entre ce sale magot et moi, quoi de
commun?', he asked. It is not simply that he and Amédée have
family ties, have both slept with Carola, fingered the same cuff-links
and had Protos as 'playmate'. In a game of difference and identity,
this antithetical image (the opposite of the '*stripling* que j'aimerais
rencontrer aujourd'hui') becomes his mirror. Both are now
alienated from their life and self. Both yearn for a past acquaintance
to put the world back in place. Both could subscribe to Amédée's
words: 'je le sens bien à présent, c'est solitaire que s'enfonce
l'obscur sentier que je suis' (p.181). And when he doubts if there
can be women 'pour caresser encore les vieillards!', how could the
youth know that his own ex-mistress has just provided that service
with genuine affection; or that, even in pulling down his beaver hat
'[qui] le séparait du paysage' (p.186), he is making himself the echo
of Amédée, so self-preoccupied on *his* journey that Protos has
commented, 'Vous n'êtes pas, je vois, très sensible aux paysages'
(p.155). In this way, Amédée is stealing his uniqueness as surely as
Julius steals the patent of his *acte gratuit*.

'Qu'il y a loin, entre l'imagination et le fait !' (p.195): a fine
description of irony. But, ironically, Lafcadio does not see its appli-
cation to his own predicament. He assumes Amédée to be a model of
smugness: hardly an accurate diagnosis of this recent victim of
Protos. And Protos, as Defouqueblize, prompts a similar

misreading: 'Encore quelque bétail pour le congrès. Pouah!' (p.218). So the imagined puppets show surprising depths, while the *subtil* simplifies, duped by his own caricatures. But the same words, proved one minute, disprove themselves the next. For, as Julius proceeds to 'fictionalize' Lafcadio, there is, indeed, *little* distance between imagination and fact. Lafcadio becomes the novelist's stooge, in a literary re-run of what he thought unique. Congratulating himself on his sang-froid after the murder, he sees this as the 'preuve que je me possède parfaitement' (p.196). But what self-possession is it, when Amédée has his hat, Protos the label and Julius his 'character'? And what 'self' does he own, when it is a far-flung amalgam of obscure motivations and contradictory tendencies? Lafcadio once scorned the retrospective alterations of literature, saying: 'C'est ce droit de retouche qui fait de l'écriture une chose si grise' (p.79). The words rebound on him, as Julius rewrites his story, and Protos 'edits' his hat. The act without an author is adopted by several, who all add their touches. Protos saps his self-esteem: 'Votre travail avait fameusement besoin de retouches, mon garçon!' (p.228). If Lafcadio felt, dressed in the 'souple et floconneuse étoffe de son complet' and his 'souples mocassins', that the *acte gratuit* meant freedom of movement, then he is disabused. And if he thought himself without links, then a mesh of consequences soon comes to join the dense psychological network in which the act was born. Gide suggests the ambivalence of his world by describing his moccasins as 'cette prison molle': a deceptive suppleness within strict limits. The paradox is that it is quite *consistent* for this 'être d'inconséquence' to arrive at the notion of a gratuitous act. It grows *necessarily* from the data of his personality. For, of all the characters, Lafcadio alone reveals his intimate past, so exposing himself to the game of psychological interpretation and supplying the means to make links and trace continuity of character. If only he could see what Gide and the reader see, he would suffer 'le sentiment de sa dépendance' (p.241) in the aftermath of his 'liberating act' all the more acutely.

The *acte gratuit*, then, is neither free nor gratuitous. Nor is it necessarily sincere, the expression of the 'real' man. But it is an immense *carrefour*, a hub of psychological directions. The pages preceding the act form a miniature 'stream of consciousness' novel: a section of inner musing, fitful, associative. Amidst the sprightly dialogues, episodic happenings and more superficial antics, this is a richly introspective passage. Like a sample of *A la recherche du temps perdu*, it wanders through dream, memory and identity, treading the frontiers of reality and idealization, and the hidden strata of the self. One could see the passageways and doors, revisited in memory, as those of an inner labyrinth; and the locks on Lafcadio's suitcase, closed or open, picked or forced, as those of the mind, with its system of springs and 'doubles fermetures'. What is it, for instance, that releases the strange premonitory image into Lafcadio's account: 'tout baigne dans une tranquillité surnaturelle; on dirait un étang où l'on va jeter clandestinement l'épervier' (p.191) – a subliminal flash as might cross the screen of a surrealist film by Buñuel? One is at the fringe of Freudian investigations, where many functions of the self meet and, to quote Rimbaud, 'JE est un autre'. It is here that mental censorship, defence mechanisms and processes of repression operate; that Lafcadio simultaneously touches and avoids his favourite images, savours and resents his past; that the actor and spectator, real and ideal selves, the man and his doubles, engage in complex dialogues. Here the subject expresses the potential conflicts of past and present, conscious and unconscious, outer and inner worlds; and reveals how one can be pulled to-and-fro, identified with but alienated from oneself, willing but resistant, one's own master and slave: 'Pourtant il n'écoutait jamais tout entier son désir et n'aimait pas céder, fût-ce à lui-même' (p.197). The act therefore allows Gide to illustrate that, in the richness of human psychology, the sources of our slightest acts are as multiple and remote as those of the Nile, and that, despite the Anthimes of the world, 'les forces de l'être et son intime météorologie restent un peu plus compliquées que vous ne les faites d'ordinaire' (*2*, p.835).

Gide's mind returned often, via different routes, to the *acte gratuit* as a psychological and intertextual *carrefour* (for further insights, see *23, 41*). It emerges notably in the ironical *soties*, as if a notion to be toyed with, a speculative or experimental possibility. In *Le Prométhée mal enchaîné* it is described as 'un acte qui n'est motivé par rien. Comprenez-vous? intérêt, passion, rien. L'acte désintéressé, né de soi; l'acte aussi sans but; donc sans maître; l'acte libre' (*1*, p.305). And in *Paludes* it gives rise to this analysis: 'ce que vous appelez l'acte libre, ce serait d'après vous, un acte ne dépendant de rien, suivez-moi: détachable – remarquez ma progression: supprimable, – et ma conclusion: sans valeur. Rattachez-vous à tout, Monsieur, et ne demandez pas la contingence; d'abord vous ne l'obtiendrez pas – et puis à quoi ça vous servirait-il?' (*1*, p.115). These two examples are adequate indication of the sustained nature of the debate. But this is not to say that Gide *believed* it, or that we in *Les Caves* (this book which questions all beliefs) are asked to believe in it, as a free act or a moral proposal. On the contrary, writing in 1929, Gide said: 'Mais non, je ne crois pas du tout, à un acte gratuit. Même je tiens celui-ci pour parfaitement impossible à concevoir, à imaginer. Il y a toujours une motivation à toute chose; mais j'entends par "acte gratuit" un acte dont la motivation n'est pas apparente, et qui présente les caractères du désintéressement. Un acte qui n'est pas accompli en vue de tel profit ou récompense, mais qui répond à une impulsion secrète, dans lequel ce que l'individu a de plus particulier se révèle, se trahit' (*1*, p.1574). So, when Lafcadio tries to say what he had against Amédée and answers, 'Je ne sais pas ... Il n'avait pas l'air heureux ... Comment voulez-vous que je vous explique ce que je ne puis m'expliquer moi-même?' (p.242), it is not that there is no explanation, but such a confusion of them at such a depth that they cannot be clarified or contained. The *acte gratuit* is the Rome one will never find the centre of, the psychological 'Mille Pattes', the deed which demonstrates that individuals' minds 'sont mieux ramifiés qu'on ne croit' (p.199). For Gide, it is an *agent provocateur*: not necessarily an end in itself, but the means of a radical challenge to metaphysical, moral, intellectual and mental assumptions. It is the perfect companion for the author who said of himself: 'Je suis un être de dialogue; tout en moi combat et se contredit' (*3*, p.547). Its presence, above all else, has enabled him to write a work of rare psychological provocation: one which denies its own appearances, belying its nature as a *sotie* led by marionettes.

6. Mirrors and 'mise en abyme'

Mirror reflections activate the text. They are rarely simple: a one-to-one encounter or act of recognition between a man and his image. When Anthime props a mirror by a cage to look at himself (p.15), his ambivalences, actual and virtual self, false atheist and closet believer, come under scrutiny. And, as mirrorer is mirrored, one wonders who is really the prisoner of conditioned reflexes, he or his rats (cf. p.125). As Anthime mocks holy images, Julie points out 'contre la glace [...] une photographie qui la représente' (p.24) and asks why *he* keeps that: a switch of focus which poses the question of *representation* (plus its reflection). Amédée's experience of blurred mirrors ('la glace était de tain sali', p.129) is synonymous with that of the dissolving identity. And, climbing a stairway, he half-glimpses *en passant* an image seen through a multiplication of frames: that of 'une glace au cadre doré' within the dirtied glass of a 'porte vitrée' (p.137). Door and mirror merge again in the railway compartment scene (p.194), when, for the vacillating Narcissus, the 'mirror' opens and swallows him up, a literal *mise en abyme*. Instead of reflecting him back, it becomes his void, projects him into infinity. In the process, landscape, the staple diet of the 'representational' artist, becomes a dance of illusions. Even Protos is seen by a window, leaning towards his reflection to adjust a false moustache in a borrowed mirror (pp.143-44): not reality, but appearances, confronted in the glass. Lafcadio questions his image: is he a Baraglioul look-alike? what figure does he cut in the eyes of the crowd? And, having examined himself in the wash-room mirror to see if he has been scratched, he is soon staring into the more complex mirror held up by Julius, where the extent to which he has been 'disfigured' and his pride wounded is posed more pointedly.

In such a context, it would perhaps be surprising if the literary work did not contain images of itself and study itself in its own mirror. The phrase *mise en abyme*, originally applied to the pictorial art of heraldry, refers to the device of incorporating into a painting a miniature reproduction of itself, so making the work, to some degree, self-referential. One result is that the onlooker, instead of passing unconsciously beyond the artistic frame into a convincing 'other world' accepted as a substitute reality, is made aware that art leads to art and is, fundamentally, its own subject. And if a tableau contains its miniature, then that miniature must also contain its miniature and so on, *ad infinitum*, in a receding play of internal self-reflection that is never exhausted, even when it disappears beyond the visible, hence the idea of the work absorbed into its own abyss. In modern criticism, the term has acquired wider connotations; but all refer to the artistic work looking inwards to contemplate its own nature. For, no less than Amédée, the book can be a Narcissus, seeking its image and definition in a host of internal mirrors more covert, fragmentary and dispersed that those consulted by its fictional creatures, the characters.

There is much discussion on the problematics of literature. Julius's novel, seen by Lafcadio, is like an 'apparition': '...frappa ses regards' (p.61). It is also 'en vitrine', seen through a glass similar to the 'porte vitrée' through which Amédée looks or the shop-window showing Lafcadio's reflection, so publicizing the novel within the novel. *L'Air des cimes* itself is a topic of debate. It has a mixed critical response, prompting Julius to say to Anthime, 'Je pensais bien qu'un tel livre ne pourrait pas vous plaire' (p.27), so raising the question, in a work as controversial and potentially offensive as *Les Caves*, of literary acceptance and moral sensitivities. What justifies or redeems a work is the problem implied by the reactions of Anthime and Juste-Agénor: 'Anthime consentirait encore à *excuser* le livre' (ibid., my emphasis), 'Si, après cela, vous n'entrez pas à l'Académie, vous êtes *impardonnable* d'avoir écrit ces sornettes' (p.44, my emphasis). Questioned in its moral *raison d'être*, the book joins the gratuity-necessity debate. (The title of a proposed text in Gide's *Paludes* is *Pléonasmes*: linguistic redundancies, with no reason for being there). Allusions to the Academy challenge literary canons and cultural legislature, and one's reason for writing. Is it to satisfy convention or explore the as yet unformulated, to pander to public approval or express the innermost tensions of the individual? Not only is 'purity' of motive tested, but the purity of literature itself: its pedigree, its place in the spectrum of high and low art. Hence the recurrent confrontation between literature and journalism: seen in the picture of Lafcadio sitting on *L'Air des cimes* while perusing a newspaper (p.62); and in the narrator's 'vous donnez dans un fait divers' (p.64), '... ne comptez pas sur ma plume' (p.75), as if his were a pure strain of writing, above the tricks of the popular press, and not that mongrel which is the *sotie*. A book's debt to father-figures is questioned by *L'Air des cimes*, 'ce livre qui n'est, à proprement parler, qu'un monument en son honneur' (p.45): a monument disowned by the father, however, as is the Vatican by the Holy Father. This reflects the ambiguous relations between Gide's own novel and moral authority or, especially, his religious upbringing: is *Les Caves* a masked tribute to his faith or a rebellion against it? It also touches the problem of the text as *monument*: as pillar of stability and reliable structure, or as 'deconstruction', shifting pattern and evasive effect. Julius queries his own position with regard to 'open' or 'closed' literature: 'Ce n'est pas maintenant qu'il venait d'achever d'écrire la vie de son père, qu'il allait se permettre des questions à son sujet' (p.49). And the fact that he does then 'undo' his book by turning against what it represents, becoming, literally, a controversial novelist, points towards a *nouveau romancier* such as Robbe-Grillet with his '*recherche* qui détruit elle-même, par l'écriture, son propre objet'.[3] Indeed, Gide incorporates many techniques of 'undoing' into his novel, not least *mise en abyme* itself, which is a subversion from within, a splitting of the novel from itself. One recalls the author's definition of 'un livre manqué' as 'celui qui laisse intact le lecteur'. Reviewing his misguided first phase, Julius sees *L'Air des cimes* as 'un livre manqué' (p.126) (one, perhaps, that leaves the author intact), and marks a rift in his literary practice.

Lafcadio is central to the debate. In claiming to hate literature

[3]*Pour un nouveau roman*, Minuit, 1963, p.74.

and to have enjoyed only *Aladdin* and *Robinson Crusoe* (p.78), he, too, puts on trial a stuffy tradition with no sense of adventure and escape. Where does *our* book sit between him and Julius, *ordre* and *aventure*, rational and imaginative, ponderous and playful? At the time of the *acte gratuit*, he predicts a catastrophe for printed books ('on foutra l'imprimé par-dessus bord'), so opening in the text the apprehension of its own crisis: the book no longer valued in familiar form and threatened as it views an abyss. Perhaps in literature, too, when true is ousted by false, the true must take on new guises in order to survive. Might one also foresee a historical moment (has it arrived in the twentieth century and is *Les Caves* its message-bearer?) when the criteria for differentiating good from bad dissolve and literature falls into an acritical void? The dilemmas of reading and writing are a constant theme. *Ecriture* as handwriting (cf. pp.59, 93, 106) surfaces like a secret code, never patent or un-equivocal. If it is worth looking into someone else's writing and for what reward is the question implicit in Lafcadio's stealing of the correspondence of a M. Gaspard Flamand (p.187). When, within this text, one peers into another, Flamand's letters or *his* diary, what does one find: sustenance or hollowness? And when Lafcadio prides himself on reading 'écriture ou imprimé, couramment, à l'envers ou par transparence, au verso, dans les glaces ou sur les buvards' (pp.189-90), he advertises the fine art of reading texts, not directly but through the mirror, back to front and upside down: an example, not just of writing aware of writing, but of a narcissistic text looking inwards at its intrinsic problems and challenging the reader's versatility in deciphering its 'indirections'.

The book is self-reflective in other ways, mirroring itself in plot, situation and expression. Lafcadio's interview with his father and Julius's with the Pope are twinned by the common verb 'incliner' (see pp.68, 177). The replay of a simple gesture – Julius's hand on Lafcadio's shoulder and Juste-Agénor's – reflects the biographer as 'chip off the old block', slave of family likenesses. Lafcadio counts to twelve before addressing his father and before the *acte gratuit*, pencilling a link between the two 'vieillards'. As the Comtesse repeats Protos's tale, Arnica's reactions are the literal duplicate of her own (see pp.103, 117), at which point Gide opens an eye and winks. Both Véronique and Amédée greet Julius with relief, hoping that his words of wisdom will save a man from ruin. Julius and Protos, independently, recite the same lines: 'Nous vivons contrefaits' (p.204), 'se doivent de vivre contrefaits' (p.225). And how could Defouqueblize know, when he says, 'Si je retournais tout de suite à mon compartiment' (p.221), that he is supported, from behind a thick textual wall, by the epigraph of Book Two: 'il ne faut jamais ôter le retour à personne' (p.43)? In the 'apparition' scenes, Anthime, Amédée and Lafcadio could be auditioning for the same part, so close are the script ('Anthime! Es-tu là?', 'Lafcadio ... Etes-vous ici?'), set ('la porte entrebâillée ... chevet du lit'), lighting ('faible lueur... diffuse clarté') and female extras ('courte forme blanche... frêle forme blanche'). And, as a last mocking image of inept travellers, Arnica and Blafaphas follow Amédée to Rome, down to the last detail of the 'missed connection' (a connection which Gide ensures that *we* do not fail to make): 'tous deux partis de Pau l'avant-veille [...] mais arrivés à Rome depuis quelques heures à peine, par suite d'un ratage de train' (p.235).

An episode, like a Russian doll, may contain its own replica. Such is the account of the midnight excursion with Wladi *within* the nocturnal journey to nowhere in the company of Amédée. For what Lafcadio conjures up, in that drowsy moment, is the recollection of *another* drowsy moment between sleep and waking: a mirroring of present and past, surface and depth. And just as the child wondered, then, 's'il n'a pas rêvé tout cela' (p.192), so, after killing Amédée, Lafcadio says, 'j'ai tué comme dans un rêve' (p.247) and asks several times 'Rêve-t-il?' (cf. pp.222, 245). During this escapade, Wladi and the boy were not just playing, but playing at playing: 'L'enfant sait bien que ce n'est là qu'un jeu, mais l'oncle y semble pris lui-même' (p.192). The compartment is a chamber of internal reflections in another way. On the wall is a photo of a seaside hotel which Amédée has been gazing at. Lafcadio also inspects it: 'je vais d'abord regarder tranquillement ce que représente cette photographie que le vieux contemplait tout à l'heure... *Miramar!* Aucun désir d'aller voir ça' (p.196). Not only does the hotel name

(Miramar / Sea View) touch on what one makes a journey to see (or not to see), and suggest an inner 'mirror' within an outer frame, but it is a model of *mise en abyme* in that, when Lafcadio says to himself, 'Let's look at what he was looking at', the answer is essentially a picture saying 'Look at'.

More elusively, there are reflections between what characters are doing or what happens in the plot, and what is happening stylistically to the text. When Julius, replying to his father's missive, stands back from his draft and tries out a phrase on his 'probité littéraire', Gide also suspends his narrative pen in an implicit plea for his own literary integrity, in this studied aside *about* Julius: 'Car Julius est une de ces nobles natures...' (p.48). In the split second that Amédée vanishes into the *gouffre*, so does the text, in the wordless gap between chapters (p.195). And when the cuff-link appears on Lafcadio's dinner-plate, it is not simply that Protos (in placing it there), Lafcadio (in slipping it under the plate) and Gide (in moving it all over the place in the book) are common masters of the ability to 'déplacer subrepticement les objets' (p.206); but that the author has, at that instant, distracted the reader and blurred his vision with a passage of heady lyricism ('Vers elle avec quelle sollicitude la mère se penche! Ah! devant de tels êtres le démon céderait...', p.222): a piece of stylistic dressing-up worthy of Defouqueblize, a verbal smoke-screen allowing him to perform *his* conjuring-trick and spring a surprise on us.

As we have seen, the characters are all reflectors of Gide the man, lurking in another sphere. Less dubiously, they are reflectors of Gide the writer, as visible on the page, as a textual presence. Julius is the obvious mirror. He is the novelist's novelist. It is he who, within Gide's fiction, dreams up a second Lafcadio; who follows his 'être d'inconséquence' at one remove; who, while sniffing the anarchic possibilities of an *acte gratuit*, stays attached to the literary life-line of a 'séquence plus subtile et cachée'. He, too, is at a literary crossroads, asks where writing lies between truth or falsity, tangles with the problem of under-motivating or over-motivating fictional characters, and, from a 'livre sans mystère ni détour', works towards the structural invitations of a *nouveau roman.*

But other figures illuminate Gide's complex authorship. Anthime and the writer are both experimenters, sending their creatures on trial runs to test their responses; and the scientist's 'compliqué système de boîtes à couloirs, à trappes, à labyrinthes, à compartiments' (p.13) resembles the book, where 'couloirs' and 'corridors souterrains', 'secrets cachots' like the Pope's dungeon, compartments of railway carriages or social hierarchy, create a commando course for neophytes of different degrees of blindness or incapacity. Gide has his own 'instruments diaboliques', sharper and more sophisticated: a malicious sense of curiosity and detour, and a 'devilish' irony for manipulating characters and readers alike. Anthime's flat, with its many rooms which 'communiquaient entre elles intérieurement' (p.23), is in the image of the book. And both character and author, in opposite styles, are blasphemers and iconoclasts, mocking the sacrosanct, taking the Lord's name in vain and mishandling holy images. Protos's role matches the narrator's. While one dupes the Countess with pseudo-historical 'corroboration', the other cons the reader with his 'il est de fait *historique*' (p.96) and 'J'avertis honnêtement le lecteur' (p.97), giving far-fetched tales *vraisemblance*. And when Amédée says, 'je suis tombé entre les mains d'un guide à qui j'ai confié ma valise et qui parlait français' (p.148), one wonders what French-speaking guide the innocent reader has stumbled upon in the textual maze. Protos mirrors the other ubiquitous master of words: through him, authorial play-acting and problems of credibility, suspect speech, imposture, bluff and double-bluff are all seen one inside the other. He sows mistrust of the written word and the unpredictabilities of the 'open' literary text: 'mais qui sait ce que peut devenir un papier?' (p.95). Both he and Gide fabricate a 'plot', are masters of the secret door, flit from place to place, adopt changes of style, exchange false confidences, divulge only not to give the game away. Both have 'des yeux bizarres, dont le regard tantôt vague et tantôt perçant commençait à [...] inquiéter' (p.226): in Gide's case, disconcerting variations of perspective, switching between the knowing and the innocent, the sly and the dead-pan, ironical acuteness and casual buffoonery.

Lafcadio's diary is a *mise en abyme*: not simply as a text within the text, but one causing Julius reading difficulties similar to our own. 'Julius tourna quelques feuillets blancs; mais un peu plus loin le carnet semblait reprendre à neuf [...] On lisait, sans plus d'indication de dates ni de lieux' (pp.55-56): for *Les Caves* also frustrates consequentiality, leaves blanks, changes tracks, abandons threads and picks them up anew, confusing time and place in a giddy *simultanéisme*. And when the *carnet* ends abruptly with the words, ' "*Comprends-tu ce qu'il y a dans ces mots*: PASSER OUTRE?" ' (p.56), a matching hiatus in Gide's script obliges a leap in the dark. Lafcadio, too, is a stylistic chameleon, swopping tones and languages, crossing linguistic frontiers. He, too, has the spirit of play, the love of detour, and a penchant for double ironic enjoyment (a *mise en abyme* in itself.): '[Il] s'amusait de lui et s'amusait à le laisser paraître' (p.78). Lafcadio and Gide both flinch (or feign to flinch) from the common herd, one physically as 'la foule l'acclamait comme un héros' (p.65), the other in his literary manner saying, 'N'attendez pas que je rapporte les propos interrompus d'une foule' (p.64). In Lafcadio's 'uncles', one sees also the image of the writer at work: 'Jongleur, escamoteur, prestidigitateur' like Baldi, showing his hand yet with tricks up his sleeve, illusionist, inventor of surprises, mimic, juggler with words; or like Wladi, shaker of the sedentary. And the problems of the *acte gratuit* are just as pertinent to that problematical act which is the book: who is the author, to whom does one trace it back, and by what tortuous routes of causality?

Details within the novel expand to become definitions of it and how it is to be read. Marguerite's reproaches to Anthime about causing scandal, and Lafcadio's revelation that, while others were shocked, his mother was amused by his running naked with a grown man, are Gide's anticipation of literary scandal: how will *Les Caves* be received by the straight-laced and those quick to moral offence? When Amédée speculates on his journey, whether it is benign and which precautions to take, it applies to the reader's journey, already underway, amidst side-tracks, wrong connections and unusual halting-places; while the phrase 'Des recherches sont faites activement le long de la voie' (p.201) mirrors those of the textual investigator. The coincidence of three characters saying 'Que signifiait cette fable absurde qui l'avait dérangé de son bonheur?' (p.172), 'vous prendrez comme vous voudrez cette aventure; moi je la tiens pour une farce qualifiée' (p.175), or 'Est-ce le fait d'un honnête homme [...] de prendre cette farce au sérieux?' (p.188) makes one scrutinize the book in the same terms: how does one take it? does one dismiss it as mere tomfoolery, a farcical extravaganza? how can a *sotie* be so disturbing? And Lafcadio's 'Belle collection de marionnettes; mais les fils sont trop apparents' (p.188) reflects, if only by its inadequacy, on Gide's art of characterization: puppets, yes, but with infinitely complex threads, requiring great dexterity to elicit such movements. The wandering cuff-links – 'reliés deux à deux [...] et taillés dans un quartz étrange, sorte d'agate embrouillardée, qui ne laissait rien voir au travers d'elle, bien qu'elle parût transparente' (p.73) – form a subtle *mise en abyme* in that the author uses his characters two by two, in complementary duets (Julius-Lafcadio, Amédée-Protos, Lafcadio-Amédée and so on), in a novel fashioned in durable materials by discipline and technique, but in a deceptively contradictory way: transparent and opaque, visible and invisible, patent and covert. Similarly, the 'Mille-Pattes' perfectly embodies the structure as a whole: not only in its 'ramifications ténébreuses' (like the underground connections of the Vatican where Pope and Truth have been literally 'mis en abîme'), but in the 'entente et ... discipline merveilleuses' (p.141) which govern it from end to end. And in the illuminated reflection of the speeding train, seen as 'une suite de carrés clairs qui dansaient le long de la voie et se déformaient tour à tour selon chaque accident du terrain' (p.194), it is not fanciful to see the image of the book, neatly divided into successive compartments, each labelled with the name of a character and clearly delineated, but within and between which images and identities are blurred in the frantic concatenations and irregular movements of the literary journey.

The novel is a system of self-referential signs. Not only of the entombed Pope might one say: 'décryptez'. *Les Caves* is a detective novel *and* its own suspect, with language the incriminating evidence. Via the subtleties of *mise en abyme*, the literary work becomes reflexive inquisition. It is literary performance and its own detailed critique: somewhat like Lafcadio, actor and insatiable spectator to itself.

7. Ironic Vision

'Tous mes livres sont *ironiques*', wrote Gide, 'ce sont des livres de critique' (*31*, p.147). By this, he does not mean essentially that they contain criticisms of society, which is more the function of satire – ridicule of follies or abuses by distortion and disguise – but that they are characterized by a critical distance, an intellectual appreciation of divergence, difference and discord, and an invitation to keep one's critical wits about one in the awareness that all is not as it seems. Irony has a knowing eye. Hence the attention drawn in *Les Caves* to one eye opening while the other stays closed (see pp.48, 103) – examples of a continuing alertness in the apparent *inconscience*, a balance of the overt and the covert. Protos, the author's double, is the arch-exponent of the half-hidden conniving look, approaching and receding: 'il reparut à la portière et [...] fermant l'œil à demi, lui fit de la main, subrepticement, signe d'approcher' (p.153).

Irony is not single-minded. It does not proceed with that blind singularity of purpose and total immersion in self which marks the behaviour of an Anthime. It stands back to take stock, weighs the for and against, and measures the discrepancies. It is duplicity of a kind, the ideal agent of Gide the double man, enabling him to be on one plane and another at the same time. It is the ironic curiosity which leads him to split characters from themselves, and feeds the technique of the duet. From the first sparring of Marguerite and Anthime – righteousness and blasphemy, breeding and coarseness, evenly matched and outscoring each other – the pattern is set. It is reiterated in the Julius-Lafcadio encounters: conversational see-saws where the initiative shifts and each has the upper hand. So, while Lafcadio smirks at Julius's embryonic *acte gratuit*, 's'amusant à reconnaître l'effet lointain de ses premiers propos' (p.204), he does not see that he is now an *effect* of the novelist's thinking; that, where he once drew his own portrait before an awed listener, a truer one is now being sketched for him; or that anti-literary man is now being made fictional. Twinned first with Blafaphas, Amédée is drawn, by the law of polarities, into a mis-match with Protos: simplicity against diversity, straight lines against deviousness. Julius and Amédée's reunion after the papal audience is a clash of ironic perspectives: the vital issue for one is an irrelevance for the other. A topsy-turvy coincidence brings Amédée together with Lafcadio: the most unlikely Baldi-substitute for the jaded appetites of the younger man. Even physical positioning makes for set-piece duos, as when Julius and Lafcadio prepare for their verbal cut and thrust: 'Julius [...] s'assit dans un fauteuil; en face de lui, Lafcadio se mit à fourchon sur une chaise' (p.205). So, too, with Lafcadio and Defouqueblize. First, 'la place en face de lui restait vide' (p.219); then the steward sits the 'Professor' there: a table for two, a spotlit theatre for a game of recognition and non-recognition between master and disciple. Gide presides over such pairings with critical aplomb, savouring the energies of debate but favouring neither side. Like Mme de Merteuil of *Les Liaisons dangereuses*, also a novel of dangerous links and antithetical characterization, he could say: 'N'est-il pas plaisant, en effet, de consoler pour et contre, et d'être le seul agent de deux intérêts directement contraires? Me voilà comme la Divinité; recevant les vœux opposés des aveugles mortels'.[4]

Opposites and humorous discrepancies bind the work. In the Anthime-Madonna contest, his flustered contortions and her spiritual quiet are set in perfect counterpoise, and the supernatural swop has a comic neatness in that the statue loses a hand while Anthime gains a leg, and as one's physical support ('la béquille') is discarded, the other's ('la tige de métal') protrudes from her broken plaster. When Lafcadio sits on Julius's open book, it is not just a snub to pedigree. It is an ironic comment on his 'unseating' of Julius in the heritage stakes; the concretization of other offhand treatments, less vulgar, of the book by father, Marguerite and press; and the source of the coincidence that while ensconced on the noble

---

[4] Livre de Poche, 1958, p.152.

work, the biography that should reveal all, Lafcadio reads the giveaway lines on the Count's illness in the cheap rag. Amédée's combat with foreign bed-bugs, of whom it is said: 'Elles ne se dirigent pas au hasard' (p.128), accentuates his own disorientated peregrinations, the quest that has gone off-target; while reverse images of the departing traveller – buoyant as he sets off refusing to let his family come to the station, and demoralized as he leaves Rome saying 'ça m'inquiète un peu de partir seul' (p.184) – eye each other sadly across the text. And what greater discrepancy is there than Julius's 'revelation' in the presence of the Pope: an impious brainwave when in the home of truth?

Ironies of situation pepper the plot: circumstances producing the wrong result or a mocking contradiction. Juste-Agénor, announcing Lafcadio's inheritance, relies on him never again to trouble the family. How can he know that the Comtesse, financially disadvantaged, will be disadvantaged again, from a new quarter, by Lafcadio's ex-associate, whose name Julius has already read in the diary; or that Lafcadio will 'trouble' or deeply disturb Julius's concept of novel-writing, Amédée's one-track life, and Geneviève's emotions and virginity? Anthime's zealous cry that 'tout ce qu'on fait au nom du Seigneur est bien fait' (p.124) already, by perfect timing or coincidence, carries the image of Protos's priestly crookery. After Carola's plea that her protégé should not be harmed, Amédée is then 'bumped off', not by the criminal whose plans he threatens, but by the indifferent Lafcadio. And when Amédée calls from the depths, 'jugez-moi, condamnez-moi, punissez-moi' (p.166), it is not God who answers him (God being as remote as the fictional Pope) but, by some random telepathy, this gratuitous justicer in an aimless world. Images show their duplicity and recur in reverse. After one bedroom visitation which brings an atheist to the faith and frees him from physical impediments, there is another which severs a believer from his faith and delivers him to the entanglements of the flesh. First it is Anthime in tears before the apparition, then it is the Virgin (as Geneviève) kneeling in tears by Lafcadio's bed. After writing one biography retrospectively about his father, Julius writes another prospectively, anticipating events, about his half-brother. And having put the Cook's ticket 'en évidence' on Julius's table, Lafcadio finds his own cuff-link 'à découvert' on his plate: a neat illustration of the switch-back of seeing, and of the ironist ironized.

Reversals of fortune or tricks of fate breed in the cracks between 'l'imagination et le fait'. Cherished notions, the best laid plans, go awry. 'Dieu me guidera jusqu'à Rome' (p.121), says Amédée, but he knows only detours and his guide is a satanic tempter. It is *because* he is reading his railway timetable that he misses his train (the guide, the Baedeker, becoming the source of error); and his 'bénigne aventure' could not be more malignant, leading as it does to his mortal malady and its 'cure' at the hands of a stranger. The virgin suffers deterioration of the flesh, the home-lover illustrates the unbearable existential loneliness of man, and the 'calme et logique esprit' (p.199) Julius, potential saviour, emerges as a raving lunatic. The same perverse hand governs Lafcadio's affairs. The man who has a horror of *debts* picks up the tab for those of his uncle: he who rejects *retouches* has his efforts corrected by a supervisor; he who is warned against the *fait divers* becomes a newspaper snippet; he who puts life over literature is fictionalized by Julius; he who scorns the 'Belle collection de marionnettes' (p.188) has his own strings pulled at that time by several people (not least by Gide who, leaving narrative for the theatrical shorthand of successive names, – JULIUS, – LAFCADIO, – JULIUS, – LAFCADIO, subjects him to a sequence of puppet-theatre). When Protos re-enters, the ex-liberator is now blackmailer; and having said 'il eût revu volontiers le gaillard qui s'était emparé de sa valise' (p.217), Lafcadio fails to recognize him when he does reappear (for the original no longer exists) and the re-seeing is most *un*welcome. Even Protos is hoist in his own petard, as his means of incriminating Lafcadio (the label) becomes the source of his own arrest and condemnation.

Emphasis on the hand of providence – 'La Providence avait bien mal loti Julius' (p.174), the 'conjoncture providentielle' (p.135) of meeting Baptistin, or the 'aventure providentielle' (p.207) which feeds Julius's novel – raises the question of who provides what for whom. For what seems to be blind fate presiding over the most inappropriate 'conjonctures' is, in fact, the all-seeing author-god, delighting in discrepancy and error. The word 'provid*ence*', from the verb *video*, makes one wonder who watches over whom, who sees on behalf of whom, and what or whom to be on the look-out for. 'J'aime à surveiller les novices' (p.228), says Protos. To see or foresee on behalf of someone is the essence of irony. It implies the interplay of one who is blind and one who is at least partially sighted. Protos is Amédée's seeing eye where naïvety cannot see for itself. And Protos's tampering with the *acte gratuit* illustrates an *oversight* in both senses: a failure to foresee by Lafcadio, and a perfect piece of supervision by Protos: a different example of one eye closed and one eye open at the same time!

The book operates on misinterpretations: errors of perspective by those who cannot read the e*vide*nce. Characters are deceived by appearances: mis-guided or mis-led as easily as Amédée is by Protos. When Amédée admits that he has not slept for three nights, Carola pinches his chin saying 'Naughty boy!': a sexual innuendo which could hardly be wider of the mark. Amédée's contact with Lafcadio is a cluster of ironies: the assumption that the lad is 'En vacances sans doute' (p.189), whereas there is a deeper sort of unemployment or 'vacancy'; the reassurance of this 'regard candide', when a voice has warned a hundred and eighty pages away, in another city and another household, and in reference to a different boyish character, that 'on eût dit un ange: c'était un aide-bourreau' (p.12); or his regret that the lad cannot speak French, a misapprehension reversed in the case of Julius who pompously translates for Lafcadio, forgetting his earlier boast that, at thirteen, he spoke four or five languages without accent. Lafcadio is just as susceptible, as the question, 'Entre ce sale magot et moi, quoi de commun?' (p.189) shows. For both have Carola as ex-mistress, embark for elsewhere, reach a dead-end and look for lost selves in a moving mirror. (And how could they know, in their non-communication, that the cuff-link worn by one, with its 'tête de chat' motif, 'communicates' with the subconscious memories of the other, where a door-knob 'en forme de tête de lion' (p.190) figures hypnotically?)

Amédée's death forms a hub of misreadings (failures to locate the author). A ticket placed on his table leads Julius to believe Amédée's fantasies and make the 'Mille-Pattes' responsible. Seeing in the death Protos's broken promise, Carola denounces him to the police. Julius says, 'Eh, bien; l'assassin est coffré' (p.241) when addressing Lafcadio himself. But it is Amédée (the one who *saw* his killer), who will no doubt misinterpret most wildly, ascribing his death to an innocent, if not non-existent Being (who, patently, was not on the spot at the time!). For, having called *de profundis* 'condamnez-moi, punissez-moi', how could he *not* see this avenging 'angel' as the hand of God, and embrace this act, an expression of 'un-necessity', as the one which, *in extremis*, restores his shattered faith in divine cause and effect? All of which are instances of judgment going off the track – as emphatically as Amédée's body.

Amidst the ironies of difference and discrepancy, one should not overlook ironic resemblances: two images of the same, as if it had acquired a double face. This may be the art of poking fun by repetition, a mimicry to mock the characters, or gentle self-mockery by Gide, playing with his textual reflections. Those involved ignore that they are repeating each other, touching the same themes or extending the implications of someone else's predicament. Lafcadio, feeling Julius's hand on his shoulder (p.203, cf. p.69), smiles at the family determinism, forgetting how *embaraglouillé* he is and that it was he who said wishfully to the father: 'm'est-il tout à fait défendu de ressembler aussi à ...' (p.69). The 'manna from heaven' for Anthime's rats and Lafcadio's windfall act in concert, as if he, too, were an experimental creature, momentarily benefited in a literary scientist's test-case. Lafcadio's and Amédée's departures tally: one sets off 'sans donner d'adresse' (p.91), the other says 'on ne saura pas où je vais' (p.120): vagabond and stay-at-home as twins, at variance but due to collide. In miniatures of the same design, Arnica and Carola stroke Amédée under the chin, but only to stress the divergence: naïve wallflower versus *femme fatale*. First the Countess faints on learning of the Pope's sequestration, then, as she narrates, Arnica passes out, falling backwards with the same weak cry and patted hands: repetitive scenarios, one affected, one sincere. Amédée's troublesome 'bouton' starts to look suspiciously like Anthime's 'loupe', 'à cet endroit honteux du cou où le bouton suspect bourgeonnait, et qu'il sentait à découvert' (p.179): a 'double-take' by which the detail itself swells in the text, exposed again when seemingly forgotten. It is an ironic graduation, after his education through the insect world via bugs, fleas and mosquitoes, that Amédée should chase the elusive habits of an organization called 'le Mille-Pattes' or centipede. The pilgrim's *voyage au bout de la nuit*, a charade of perils and false alarms, is a pathetic replica of Lafcadio's with Wladi. And what is a more subtle coincidence than Defouqueblize's speech on the subject of 'une simple interruption de courant' (p.226), in view of the fact that, of Amédée's hotel in Genoa, we are told (though in a parenthesis, as if not quite attaining full textual status), '(L'éclairage était électrique, qu'on arrêtait en chavirant la chevillette d'un interrupteur de courant)' (pp.132-33); and that, in the railway compartment, Amédée has tried to avoid the inevitable – 'Fleurissoire tourna le commutateur' (p.193) – by throwing a light-switch. Fine examples of a 'séquence plus subtile et cachée'; and of a versatile mimicry or art of *ressemblance* like that of Baldi who, among other talents, 'dansait, cabriolait' (p.85), not unlike Lafcadio's new 'playmate' Amédée, whose pliable outlines are seen, finally, to do the same thing, the docile pupil of the missing master: 'On apercevait [...] *danser* l'ombre falote de Fleurissoire [...] l'ombre du Chinois *cabrioler*' (pp.194-95, my emphasis).

Among the commonest expressions of irony is for language to say one thing and mean another, for language itself (like the characters) to wear masks. Protos is a fount of examples. That he can flatter the Comtesse that 'votre foi n'était point de ces fois mondaines' (p.95) when he is the embodiment of faithlessness; that he can belittle others' faiths as 'simple revêtements de l'indifférence' (ibid.) when he is a wolf in priest's clothing; that his story can concern a *mannequin* usurping religious power, when every detail applies to him; that he, the slippery speaker, can turn the tables by saying 'j'ai dans votre généreuse parole la confiance la plus entière' (p.103) and suspect his victim of 'de la tiédeur [...] et presque de la duplicité' (p.105); that he can slip 'involuntarily' into Spanish, exclaiming 'la sincérité de mes sentiments me trahit', only to be reassured by his dupe that 'vous parlez le français avec une pureté...' (p.106): are prime illustrations of the two-faced nature of language, revelling in deceptiveness.

Protos is irony's front man, but language needs no help as an agent of double (or plural) meanings. When Amédée gasps to Carola, 'Ouvrez un peu la fenêtre' (p.138), this is the very service which Lafcadio will ultimately provide for him! And when Lafcadio asks, 'D'où sort cet étrange vieillard?' (p.189), the answer might be the cocoon of the Fleurissoire household, the same family tree as Julius, the germinating powers of Protos's fiction, or, prospectively, the carriage door! Julius's election, in which 'l'Académie venait à lui, *portes ouvertes*' (p.234, my emphasis), frees similar ironic resonances: not only is the Institution a 'closed shop' and an end to Julius's 'open' life, but we know what the phrase has meant, literally, for Amédée. When Bardolotti, seeing Amédée's sickness, offers help, saying, 'Vous êtes tout sali' (p.166), his words, following 'quelle extraordinaire pénitence me *lavera* de ce crime extraordinaire?' (ibid., my emphasis), set up a grotesque clash of literal and figurative: a pseudo-priest giving 'absolution' (or ablution) by offering to mop him down with a towel. Nor is it accidental that Defouqueblize should introduce himself to Lafcadio as professor in a newly established Chair of 'criminologie comparée' (p.225). For he has just made himself the student of Lafcadio's 'crime', enabling us to compare two criminologies, his on the grand scale and Lafcadio's individual one; while Lafcadio, in differentiating 'crime' from 'aventure' (p.200), has also been indulging, in another sense, in an exercise of 'criminologie comparée'.

Such examples could be continued *ad infinitum*, and lead to a wider study of the game of language. It suffices to say that irony, operating at many levels, surfacing and disappearing, creates an elaborate network, alive with echoes and reverberations. It has endless 'corridors souterrains'. The reader, on his journey, traces these connections, with a smile of recognition: in this book where recognition is everybody's difficulty. Rather than the laugh, irony cultivates the knowing *sourire*: *sub-ridere*, the laugh beneath the surface, *sous cape* or 'sous enveloppe', born of and thriving on disguise.

8. The Play of Language

Les Caves is a compendium of games. Lafcadio learns chess from Baldi, as well as whist and the art of cheating. As a child he could play without looking at the board, as if above laws of compartments and the strictures of the frame; and before killing Amédée he shuns circumspection saying, 'Et pas plus le droit de reprendre son coup qu'aux échecs' (p.195). Amédée's death becomes a numbers game, where Lafcadio juggles the figures or loads the dice in his favour. He carries the dice of a 'jeu de tric-trac' (p.197) as a talisman from Baldi, and uses it to decide directions (though he does not feel obliged to respect the number thrown, so leaving the game of *disponibilité*, chance and necessity, more open). The *acte gratuit* resembles 'cligne-musette', a version of hide-and-seek or blind man's buff (one thinks of Amédée with Protos): will he be found out or not? Baldi was also a juggler (see p.85), making fanciful patterns with everyday objects. In follow-my-leader with Wladi, Lafcadio is 'en appétit d'amusement' (p.191) and, even if the suspense is rigged, 'il se prête au jeu'. The uncle displaces the boy's 'sac de billes' (p.190) on his bedside table for no apparent reason: a possible sign of the spirit of play and the unpredictable trajectories, collisions and deflections of the book. Julius's and Lafcadio's verbal one-upmanship on the *acte gratuit* is a game of leapfrog: 'Ainsi tour à tour bondissant et dépassant, [...] on eût dit que l'un jouait à saute-mouton avec l'autre' (p.206). This, too, reflects a novel where characters, as at chess or ludo, jump over each other, move alternately ahead or behind, or meet uncomfortably in the same squares. So that when Protos says to Amédée, 'Quoi! votre intention pouvait-elle être de l'aller trouver tout de go?' (p.149), one sees a similar game half-hiding its identity, a game, as it were, pretending not to be a game: Japanese *go*, a complicated board-game of multiplying movements, positional dilemmas and greater or lesser degrees of liberty.

Gide's 'appétit d'amusement' is no less than Lafcadio's. The phrase 'Il s'amusait à...' is irrepressible. When Lafcadio says, 'Ce sera sûrement beaucoup moins sage, mais peut-être un peu plus amusant' (p.199), it mirrors Gide's artistic mood: the ebullient, mercurial style after the more introverted soul-searching of *La Porte étroite* or *L'Immoraliste*. It shows how being *diverted* or side-tracked, and being entertained, are the same. For just as Baldi frees things to a new value, 'distante de toute utilité' (p.85), so is the spirit of play non-utilitarian, indulged in for its own sake. The novel so inspired becomes, in large measure, an *acte gratuit*: performed, whatever its deeper motives and hidden structures, with no greater end in mind than the joy of its own performance. The second chapter begins: 'Le jubilé était tout proche' (p.14). Is this the author thinking aloud on the verge of his fiction, relishing (since the jubilee is dated 1893, a liberating date in Gide's life) the prospect of his own novelistic high spirits, far from 'ceux qui cherchent en gémissant' (p.127): an amused escape from himself, especially with regard to a religious subject?

The *sotie* is a carnival of play-acting, a costumed festival in which the novelist is not upstaged. One is treated, from the outset, to the histrionics of style: over-emphasis, exaggeration, contrived phrasing, archaic pretence – all part of the 'dressing-up' of language. Anthime's opening 'ton de commisération renchérie' is matched by the author's own: 'et c'était certes grand-pitié que de voir ce vaste corps à demi perclus occuper à cette parodie le reliquat de ses disponibilités musculaires' (p.9) (human and *literary* parody as one, where the playful stylization undermines what it pretends to express). Armand-*Dubois*, the most wooden character closest to puppetry, also funds Gide's most patent melodrama. The mason's show-down with the statue is a feast of stagy effect, where the jerkiness of strip-cartoon, the suspense of serial and a dose of gothic horror compete for the author's pen: 'Le séraphique éclairement du soir, apaisant son âme rebelle, l'inclinerait peut-être... Mais non: il échappe au conseil [...] Parfois un gémissement échappe à ses lèvres tordues; ses traits se convulsent. Où le mène sa rage impie? [...]

penché sur lui, que dit-il, qui fasse tressaillir l'enfant? – Non! non! le petit proteste' (pp.32-33). Such theatricality is contagious. There is 'sob stuff' as the *dramatis personae* clutch at hankies (pp.94, 99, 245, etc.), and slapstick as Defouqueblize drops pince-nez and crushes top hat (p.219). But it is refined by the author's 'hanky-panky'. For, into the sham of the 'weepies', he slips a more intellectual game of repetitions and recognitions; and, into the physical clowning, tricky subterfuges of his own. More generally, Gide exploits stylistic mimicry, adapting his tones and tempos, like a good *subtil*, to the characters' speech, antics and idiosyncrasies (see, for example, p.30). The *style indirect libre* is an ideal expressive medium for the volatile author: allowing him to slide fluently between self and other, narrative exposition and character's point of view. He can be simultaneously without and within, distant and close, enjoying (like Protos) tricks of displacement, inventive *disponibilité* (committed but not committed) and the mixing of roles. Gide's pen is master of any part, switching in and out, impersonating any voice. With a twist of syntax, a phonetic reinforcement, it can adjust the lighting, alter a tone. That this is done with literary self-awareness is indicated, not only by references to people's writing styles, but as Julius (author) stands back from a press report to cast a critical eye on its forced excesses of style: '*Il a apparemment été projeté du wagon, assez violemment pour passer par-dessus le parapet du pont, en réparation à cet endroit et remplacé simplement par des poutres.* (Quel style!)' (p.208). In this double language game – enjoyed both in the phoney plethora of plosives and its satirical deflation – is not Gide, in parenthesis, saying of his own performance: 'Quel style!'

The author's 'sac de billes' is his bag of words. Perhaps they are made of the same cloudy agate as the wandering cuff-links, seemingly transparent yet not transparent, and blurring the issue as they roll about. The question of how many foreign languages one speaks applies to Lafcadio *and* the reader. *Les Caves* is a hive of foreign words, English, Italian, German: causing a *dépaysement*, making the familiar less familiar, offering translations of the same. They urge the reader (like Gide who, in his own life, left the restrictive vision of one culture) to cross frontiers, *passer outre*, move between less and more obscure. They are a game of masks: reality in another guise, making significance complex and mobile. Language becomes a crossroads, not only geographically, but as a meeting-point of multi-directional references. So, the 'via dei Vecchierelli' (p.135) where Amédée's boarding (or bawdy) house is located, is the 'street of the little old men': oddly prophetic in view of Lafcadio's 'd'où sort cet étrange vieillard?' (p.189) and 'petit vieux du wagon' (p.207). That the street is the *third* street past a bridge (echoed, in a Lafcadio-like numbers game, by Amédée's room being on the third floor and the third door down the corridor) connects with Anthime's 'madone tri*vi*ale', and stamps Carola, too, as a 'madonna of the three ways', or 'the third street' (linked with Lafcadio, Protos and Amédée in turn). And does one see, in the plural 'vecchierelli', the routes of *three* old men: Anthime, Julius and Amédée, going variously to Rome? When Lafcadio says, 'ces vieillards sont mieux ramifiés qu'on ne croit' (p.199), his thought is that many roads lead off Amédée and that he cannot 'démêler quelle parenté ou quels rapport entre Julius et ce vieux'. But can one fathom or unravel any more easily the obscure parentage and complex relationships of language? For the very words 'via dei vecchierelli' part in as many directions. Lafcadio's 'Ce vieillard est un carrefour' (p.201) is almost their direct translation. Is it surprising that Protos, wishing secrecy, should shout at his servant, 'Allez-vous-en. Via! Via!' (p.161), scattering this seme in the air? Its seed was floating even in the first chapter, telling us that Anthime lived in the 'via in Lucina' (p.10): an inappropriate setting for his obscurantism, and an ironic preview of Amédée's trek from light to dark.

Protos's request to Fleurissoire to go to the 'Credito Commerciale de Rome' (p.167) is a similar linguistic complex: a tie for all the notions of credibility, credos, credence, credit and discredit running through the text. It interlocks financial operations and belief, and is a synonym of Protos's crooked enterprise, founded on what one believes about Rome. (Both Lafcadio's uncle, with his tailor's bills, and Protos have, in different ways, been living on credit.) It is equally a synonym for Amédée's credulous Roman journey of faith, inseparable from his accounting: 'il fait ses comptes et ses prières'. It harks back also to Anthime's faith, exploited by Rome ('head office') for financial gain. Protos, significantly, changes disguises again at the end of this episode: from priest to bank employee (p.168) – an easy accommodation of God and Mammon, already sanctioned by the double-barrelled name of the Comtesse de *Saint-Prix*.

A final example of the underground adventures of the foreign phrase is the English poetry (mis)quoted by Lafcadio as he sinks into sleepy despair: '*My heart aches; a drowsy numbness pains / My senses*' (p.245). Not only do Keats's lines veil and reveal the irony that Lafcadio is the dilettante he claims not to be; that, even when crying alone, he is acting for himself with borrowed speech and romantic affectation; that sincerity is a semblance, trailing self-conscious models and stylized images; and that, as well as tears, he enjoys the narcissism of a literary mirror. More relevantly, the language itself becomes self-mirroring, in that the poetry can be found translated, word for word, in the French one has just read (perhaps without noticing): 'une torpeur étrange engourdissait désespérément sa pensée [...] son cœur [...] lui faisait mal' (ibid.). So, the text communicates with its foreign double. One is even less likely to have noticed that the same translation has been there, with a time fuse, since the Virgin's apparition to Anthime: 'une extraordinaire mollesse l'engourdit [...] une sorte de torpeur étrange' (pp.35-36). Indeed, the marbles have rolled under many beds!

The names of characters are also a foreign language to be translated. They, too, have a deviant genealogy and hidden identities. They, too, go roaming textually. The name Baraglioul is as tortuous as its family tree (p.20), caught between *embarras*, *embrouiller* and *baragouiner*: confusion, mix-ups and the obscurities of language. And the Juste-Agénor prefix is a tempting echo of *à genoux*, suggesting genuflexions before the holy father, or Anthime's and Lafcadio's postures before Madonna or paterfamilias (see pp.37, 72). Protos's reference to the *Campo dei Fiori* gives a sideways nudge to the name *Fleuri*ssoire, and to the dotty botanist's

own 'field of flowers': his three daughters, Véronique, Marguerite
and Arnica. Their maiden name Péterat (pétera = will fart) is
literally deflationary, creating odoriferous 'fleurs du mal'; while the
nickname *les Blafafoires* (blafard = pallid, foire = fun-fair) suggests
pasty-faced clowns, anaemic figures of fun whose lives are a comic
shambles, if not an unsavoury mess (foire = diarrhœa). Baptistin's
appearance as advance guide to the city of faith conjures up John the
Baptist, though here heralding a dubious Messiah or deliverer,
namely Protos; while the idea of baptism and the bearing of
Christian names is picked out by a mention of going through 'un
labyrinthe de ruelles *sans nom*'(p.136, my emphasis). And, as if to
alert us to the 'goings on' at the borders of language, the hidden
meanings, cross-references and *quiproquos*, Baptistin takes Amédée
to a house 'où des dames très complaisantes parlent toutes les
langues' (p.135). The name Carola *Venitequa* ('Come here', the
opposite of Protos's 'Via! Via!') captures her 'come hither' charms.
An odd detail is that Amédée, on the stairs, notices the word *Salone*
on the dirtied glass of a door near a mirror '[qu'il] ne distinguait
qu'à peine' (p.137). Is it far-fetched to imagine, in view of the
Grazia/Grazie one-letter error on the previous page, that what he
really saw was *Salome*; and that seduction by a temptress governs
the death of this one-man servant of religious truth who has gone
ahead to light the way, like John the Baptist?

On, finally, to the flush of Cardinals, including the ironically
named 'cardinal San-Felice' (p.145) in a book where religious
patronage brings only frustration and misery. One figures more (but
perhaps less) prominently than others: 'cardinal André'. The
Comtesse, we are told, 'tient le cardinal André dans sa manche et,
partant, les quinze immortels qui toujours votent avec lui' (p.27).
Anthime's conversion leaks out via Cardinal André 'qui l'ébruita
dans le parti conservateur' (p.38), and it is he who promises to
promote the convert's case with the Church (p.46). Protos worms
his way into the Countess's trust using the same name (p.93). And it
is the same dignitary who finally informs Julius of his election to
the Academy (p.234). Might one suspect another case of two
identities under one name, and more literary hide-and-seek: *our*

André, the omnipresent link-man, with influence in high places, controlling the issue of literary exclusion and admission, obscurely involved with secrets that leak out, false credentials, promises that are not kept, support which is not as trustworthy as it seems, and the question of what or whom one has up one's sleeve (or eating out of one's hand)? It is no accident that the library where Lafcadio consults the *Who's Who?* is the 'bibliothèque Cardinal' (p.60). Protos gives Amédée an envelope 'où il venait d'inscrire l'adresse apocryphe du cardinal' (p.151): a text of dubious authorship and authenticity (like Julius's novel). When one reads of Bardolotti that 'le cardinal, en se passant la main sur le visage, en dépouilla d'un coup la profane et factice gaieté' (p.161), the title becomes synonymous with false faces. And as Protos fades away muttering ominously, 'On t'en donnera, du cardinal!' (p.152), one half-hears Gide promising the reader the same thing: a plentiful dose of cardinalitis, from the *quatre vertus cardinales* (courage, justice, prudence and temperance, all of which Amédée loses along the way, thanks to the ministrations of 'priests'), to the *quatre points cardinaux* (the points of compass, to which the characters' directions and the book's journey-patterns are confusingly scattered).

Another form of linguistic play, and name-dropping of a kind, is the use of literary allusion. This goes further than broad literary parody, the mocking replay of clichés of the genre (though the *protean* Gide turns his hand to brief set pieces of *roman fleuve*, gothic melodrama, spy thriller, romantic novelette, cloak and dagger serial, puppet theatre and so on, trying on everything in the literary costume-shop). Nor is it simply situational resemblances: Anthime's conversion as a replica of that of Saul, falling to the ground, with a light from heaven shining about him, and a voice saying, 'Why persecutest thou me?'; or Amédée as bumbling Don Quixote lunging at enlarged mosquitoes on his picaresque travels as the Spanish hero tilted at windmills; or Lafcadio's voice in the night, like the divine call to the boy Samuel, speaking his name a second and a third time, '– Lafcadio... Etes-vous ici, Lafcadio?' (p.245). Beyond this lies a trickier network of literary quotation:

more elusive tracings of intertextuality. Is this surprising in a book where a novelist plagiarizes a character; where others' texts are furtively opened for diversion, and there is pleasure in prying into the wider world of 'letters'? A small sample from nineteenth-century French classics indicates that here, too, heredity can be tenacious. The description of Anthime hunched demoniacally in his laboratory, amidst a labyrinth of landings, doors and corridors, is a copy of Grandet in Balzac's *Eugénie Grandet*: 'Personne, pas même Madame Grandet, n'avait la permission d'y venir [...] Lui seul avait la clef de ce laboratoire'.[5] Apart from the broader themes of aristocracy of spirit versus vulgarity, the cult of the *imprévu* or escape from moral asphyxia, Lafcadio takes his cue on several occasions from Julien in Stendhal's *Le Rouge et le Noir*: 'faites toujours le contraire de ce qu'on attend de vous', 'Il prit un grand détour'. [6] And Lafcadio's glimpse of the 'widow's' leg is surely a teasing replay of Baudelaire's *A une passante*: 'Longue, mince, en grand deuil [...] / Une femme passa [...] / Soulevant, balançant le feston et l'ourlet; / Agile et noble, avec sa jambe de statue/ [...] Un éclair... puis la nuit!' These are but a few of the cryptic clues in a game of hunt the thimble which may prove as fruitless as Amédée's efforts to track down the evasive.

Reminders to beware of words are everywhere: notably the word *Cave* itself with its warning in disguise and plural meanings (cellar, hollow, dupe, straight-man). There is much haggling or hair-splitting over words which asks the reader also to discriminate, not to take a word for granted as the inalterable expression of itself. When Julius asks of Anthime 'des nouvelles de sa sciatique, qu'il appelle par erreur: son lumbago' (p.27), one is alerted to the deviations of language, slipping fractionally awry. Lafcadio measures linguistic divergence, in his 'dis-crimin-ations' over the words *crime* and *criminel* and possible variants. Julius's chat with Marguerite about his book's bad press shows how one word, inserted or omitted, can change the tenor of a text, and encourages

---

[5] Livre de poche, 1972, pp.70-71.

[6] Garnier, 1960, pp.276, 389.

vigilance with regard to the 'accidents' of language (see p.46). He takes *punta* in Lafcadio's diary to be something other than it is: a word open to more or less utilitarian readings. Not only Baldi's variable face, but language 'parts from itself' – 'se départait de toute ressemblance avec lui-même' (p.85) – the victim of its own *écart*. Protos warns of the precariousness of language, its pitfalls and unpredictabilities – 'Et souvenez-vous qu'un mot de vous peut tout perdre' (p.106) – and how words can depart into an abyss of further implications: 'Ah! si je lui disais [...] où ils vont de ce pas rapporter nos moindres paroles!' (p.162). One is strategically reminded of the problematics of language. Lafcadio asks Julius, who has ferreted in his cryptic notebook: 'Je voudrais bien savoir si vous avez également lu un bout de lettre qui se trouvait dans le carnet?' (p.78). Julius hasn't, because he did not find it. Nor do we: we never know what it is, nor what its significance might or might not have been. It is a tantalizing missing dimension: the lure of the absent text. Amédée suffers from language in a half-and-half world. In reply to Bardolotti's 'vous m'entendez à demi-mot, cher Monsieur', he puts on a brave show of connivence: 'Fleurissoire eut un fin clin d'œil. S'il l'entendait à demi-mot! oui, certes et point n'était besoin de le redire; mais en vain cherchait-il quelque phrase qui pût à la fois ne rien dire et tout signifier' (p.160). While stressing the role of hints and tacit understandings. this exchange shows Amédée's nostalgia for the perfection of the Word: that ever-elusive formula which would be the reconciliation of utterance and silence, total meaning and absence of meaning. And it is perhaps only Gide, as 'divine artist' or creator-god. who commands such expression, beyond the inept gropings of his characters and even the ingenuities of the forked tongue of Protos. When Amédée espies Julius in Rome, their meeting undergoes a double distanciation or alienation affecting language. As for Julius, talking to himself as he walks, 'si le froissement du jet d'eau couvrait le bruit de ses paroles, du moins distinguait-on ses lèvres s'agiter' (p.173). And Amédée has brought back from his previous day's excesses 'un enrouement mystérieux, de sorte que semblaient venir de loin ses paroles' (p.174). The effect is not simply a *dialogue de sourds*, but a divorce or partial disconnection between speech and its origins, language and its author, as if the link had become tenuous.

Language, in *Les Caves*, is not univalent, any more than the self. It has difficulty in *being itself*. It becomes, as if involuntarily, an agent of plural meaning. Like Amédée, it loses its innocence, where innocence means attachment to one reliable connotation. So, Julius's disclosure that 'Anthime a été joué, que tous nous sommes joués' (p.178) signifies, not just that they are being hoodwinked, but that they are all false characters, playing parts, all part of a game (as the phrase itself is a part of a game). When Blafaphas asks about macaroni, saying *'Je suis sur le chemin d'une nouvelle découverte'* (p.172), other roads to discovery, more *embrouillés* than macaroni and more serious, come to mind. When Julius, viewing his broken finger-nail, sees that 'le mal était irréparable [...] plus rien à faire qu'à couper' (p.243), one thinks of the irredeemable sin on Amédée's conscience, the irreparable *acte gratuit*, and other things summarily cut off, like Amédée's life.

The text is alive with verbal echoes: words not content with a single identity but leading a double life. The same but not the same, they also say: 'quoi de commun?' Juste-Agénor and Lafcadio mimic each other from afar (see pp.43, 188). Protos echoes himself in his show-down with Lafcadio: 'la police [...] compose avec les subtils. "Compose", oui, je crois que c'est le mot [...] vous soumettez-vous?' (p.231, cf. p.98). (The reader or critic, in *his* police-work, has to 'compose' with the *subtils* in a different, literary sense). Similarly, Protos's catch-phrase 'Je prends mon élan' (p.87) slyly reappears, not from his own mouth, but in Gide's description of Defouqueblize: 'Defouqueblize, à ces mots, prit une sorte d'élan comme pour abandonner sa chaise' (p.226). The reader may sit up in his seat, in recognizing *these* words. For, even with *subtils*, who never in theory repeat themselves, there are secret continuities. Many characters are heard to groan (see pp.103, 116, 118), unaware that they are lending weight, in another textual dimension, to the epigraph of Book Four: *'Et je ne puis approuver que ceux qui cherchent en gémissant'* (p.127). Protos voices exactly what Amédée has been thinking: 'Une sorte [...] de pressentiment, d'avertissement intérieur...' (p.135), 'je ne sais quel pressentiment, quel avertissement d'en haut...' (p.146). A 'conjoncture providentielle', indeed! Lafcadio's last words before vanishing are 'N'importe' (p.73); while the first that Amédée hears from Julius as he resurfaces in Rome are 'QUE NOUS IMPORTE!' (p.173): a bizarre underground life, as if characters were carried on the capricious connections of words. After the *acte gratuit*, the narrator says of Lafcadio:

> Il courut à son compartiment.
> Ah! combien, devant l'étrangeté d'un fait, l'exclamation semble inutile! Plus surprenant est l'événement et plus mon récit sera simple. Je dirai donc tout net ceci: Quand Lafcadio rentra dans le compartiment pour y reprendre sa valise, la valise n'y était plus.
> Il crut d'abord s'être trompé, ressortit dans le couloir.
> (p.198)

If one goes back through the labyrinth, what does one find? Answer: Anthime's maze, with its 'couloirs' and 'compartiments', 'contenant les uns la nourriture, les autres rien' (p.13) – not even a suitcase! Nor does the game end here. For, in dismissing exclamations as useless, the narrator uses two, so not practising what he preaches or, like Lafcadio, infringing his own rules. And this is hardly *simple* writing, given the far-flung echoes and the fussy rhetorical insert to *tell* us that the narrative is now being stripped of frills. One final example stands for a myriad. Having received the cuff-links from Carola (p.152), Amédée smartens up to meet Julius: 'Du moins prit-il soin de retourner ses manchettes; quant au col, il le recouvrait de son foulard, ce qui présentait en outre cet avantage de cacher à peu près son bouton' (p.172). So, by subliminal advertising, the word 'bouton de manchette' flashes by, even though 'bouton' has another meaning, his inflamed spot. And, as if the time is still not ripe for the ultimate connection of parts, Lafcadio watches Amédée struggling with a collar-stud: 'le col enfin admit le bouton. Fleurissoire reprit alors [...] près [...] de sa veste et de ses manchettes, sa cravate' (p.194). So, when he does exclaim, on reading the newspaper ('que je traduis', says Gide the *translator*), 'Quoi! les boutons de Carola maintenant! Ce vieillard est un carrefour' (p.201), not only is the old man a crossroads, but also the word 'cufflinks'.

We are led into alleys of linguistic links: not precise repetitions, but secret affiliations. (And where, as with the *acte gratuit*, do such connections begin and end?) Who could predict, seeing the Madonna's outstretched hands ('ses mains offertes'), that a plaster hand will be given, at a 'knock-down' price, and carried off in Anthime's pocket? How can one know that the 'Madone triviale' prefigures three routes to Rome and Gide's tripartite treatment of the 'adventures' of Anthime, Julius and Amédée? And as the Virgin raises 'sa manche vide' (p.36) to the disbeliever, is it far-fetched to see, in *his* alcove, the authorial miracle-worker with tricks up his sleeve? When Julius, sceptical of cardinal André's help, says, 'Voilà qui me fait une belle jambe!' (p.46), we think back to Anthime's 'new leg', supplied by a different religious agency. Amédée's musings on the insect-repellent night-lights called *fidibus* (p.133) invented by Blafaphas Snr. stir other declensions of the word 'faith' (*fidèles, infidèles, se fier, confier, confiance, ma foi*), also designed to give protection in the dark. But is one more effective than the other, with its 'abondance de fumée narcotique' (opium of the people?) which half-asphyxiates the sleeper while shielding him? So, as one reconsiders the mysteries of names, what seemed an idle reminiscence joins a mesh of references binding the text.

In order to feign innocence with Amédée as someone passes by, Protos goes off on a side-track about cigarette-smoking: 'Voilà pourquoi ces *Virginias*, si appréciés de certains fumeurs [...] Un *Virginia* qui ne tire pas bien n'est bon qu'à jeter' (pp.146-47). The words are a smoke-screen, for Protos *and* for Gide, mingling with the 'fumée narcotique' and with Blafaphas's 'pipe fumivore hygiénique, pour fumeurs délicats' (p.112). And, far from being pure irrelevance, they are contaminated with meaning: the potency of the 'Sainte Vierge' for Anthime; the virgin Arnica not yet deflowered in marriage; the pilgrim's loss of virginity with Carola; the 'feuille vierge' (p.150) in Protos's notebook. And the 'spotless' Fleurissoire does prove a dead loss, does not 'draw' well (financially) and is only fit to be thrown away. As Amédée stifles, Carola says, 'On va le pousser près de la *croisée*' (p.138, my emphasis): a word which, though meaning 'casement window', jostles with 'le mot *croisade*' (p.119, my emphasis) and with 'ce *croisé* naïf' (p.142, my emphasis) who is Amédée, masculine and feminine of the same word, married but apart. Protos produces a copy of the periodical *La Croix* (p.164): a one-word *carrefour* close to *croisée des chemins* or *croisement de la route*, as well as the *chassé-croisé* of crossed paths and changing partners, and the *mots croisés* of which this is a literal example.

It is in a villa 'sur les pentes du Vomero' (p.150), a Naples suburb close to lava-spewing Vesuvius, that Amédée meets Bardolotti: a linguistic trigger to his 'sickness unto death' ('il commença par rendre son déjeuner', p.165). Protos, out of the blue, buys a lottery ticket and appears with 'un gros dindon plumé' (p.156) under his arm: gratuitous, or is it? For is not Fleurissoire the 'dindon de la farce', the comic simpleton, in the chancer's pocket if not under his arm, as predicted by Carola: 'Crois-moi, ma pauvre poule, il va te plumer' (p.170)? When Amédée, with Julius, finds that 'tout [...] reprenait poids rassurant' (p.173), one recalls the weighing of the rats fed by Véronique, and other unlikely questions of weights and measures, like Blafaphas's invention of a 'pèse-billes' (p.112), suggesting again how carefully one has to weigh, not merely marbles, but words. Protos has said: '*Cave* est un mot latin qui veut dire aussi: PRENDS GARDE!' (p.151) – a *mise en abyme* where the word which says beware is what to beware of. As if to prove it, the phrase recurs in a new context, from a new source (the narrator) and with a new recipient (Lafcadio): 'Il ne prenait pas garde à ceci' (p.185). Such linguistic displacements are a test of the reader as *crustacé* or *subtil*. *Jeux de mots* and *jeu de sots* are one. Like Carola's costume ('recouvrait... signalait'), they advertise and disguise. An interesting P.S. rounds off Juste-Agénor's letter to Julius: '*Ne laissez point paraître que vous venez de ma part*' (p.44):

the sign of a text which plays hide-and-seek, and an author who, like Lafcadio literally, does not wish to give the game away.

There is an academic rumour abroad that the word 'sincere' derives from the Latin 'sine + cera' ('without wax'), and has its origins in statuary, where a statue with no wax was a product of best credentials. In a work like *Les Caves*, which explicitly debates the value of a statue and the materials it is made of (see p.32), and where reference is made to the *wax* seal on Lafcadio's secrets, to the fact that Julius breaks his prize finger-nail while scratching 'une petite tache de bougie' from the table-cloth, and to a fraudulent personage called '(San) Ciro' (cf. 'la cire'), one might ask if this is not another recondite language game, threaded through the crucial theme of sincerity, more obviously illustrated in its waxworks characters. Or is this another instance of words which are there and not there, of a false track dependent (in its dubious etymology) on a one-letter error and the confusion of masculine and feminine, and of a plausible fabrication like Protos's, ultimately without foundation?

9. Temptation and Salvation

The juggling, the word-bending, the flippancy, the ironic peek-a-boo, do not disguise that *Les Caves du Vatican*, though playfully sacrilegious, is a work of deep spiritual enquiry. If crossroads and crosswords are its hallmark, so is the sign of the Cross. On one level, it is a topical work. The 1890s, fired by the annexation of Vatican possessions by the Italian government, were a time, in a sensitive post-Dreyfus France, of controversy and tension between Church and State. Catholicism mounted a crusade for support; the papal image (though Cardinal Rapallo and others) became unusually linked with political manoeuvring, financial backing and commercialism. Relations between freemasonry and the faith were suspicious, with fear of double agents. There was pressure to 'come out' and declare oneself: religious allegiances came under surveillance, with political vetting and questions as to one's real or apparent Catholic affiliations. Such a backdrop provides an active setting for the terms of Gide's debate, reflects the personal ambiguities which led him to say, 'Le catholicisme est inadmissible. Le protestantisme est intolérable. Et je me sens profondément chrétien' (*2*, p.367), and foreshadows his own temptation, pressed by the poets Claudel and Jammes, towards a Catholic conversion, in the war years following the publication of *Les Caves*.

But the concerns of the work cut deeper than historical atmospherics or wrangles of Church and Lodge. Its opening dialogue, an exhortation to Anthime to repent and return to the path of righteousness, focuses on the sickness of the soul. Though humorously staged, the dialectic of the angelic and the diabolical already binds the thematic fabric. Armand-Dubois as 'faux dieu' embodies the sin of pride and man's deluded aspirations to divinity; while his scientific blueprints, however ludicrous, trace the serious question of how to get to grips with God. The good-evil axis structures the book: in the atheist's fulminations versus the Madonna's seraphic grace, in Amédée's tug-of-war between malignant and benign, and in the *acte gratuit*, which transcends good and evil and probes the reasons for saving or losing a life. Carola, though a cliché of the good-hearted prostitute and gangster's moll, illustrates the battle of corruption and purity in the human heart, in terms worthy of the author of *Les Fleurs du Mal* (see p.143). And, though a servant of *le Malin*, her maternal attachment to Amédée's innocence leads Gide to speculate on the stirrings of an 'âme qui se révolte', perhaps not irredeemable. Fleurissoire symbolizes man after the fall, unable to distinguish vice and virtue, real and apparent sin, in a topsy-turvy world where the malicious seem only to be feigning sinfulness, while he, the pure of heart, is stained by it in fact.

Protos's role is crucial. This shifty figure, while representing appearances, reality on the move and anti-truth, is just as easily a manifestation of the Devil. It is he who questions the authority and authenticity of the Father, and undermines from within institutions of the faith, turning truth into falsity. Picking out prodigal sons, he takes the unwary and calls them from the path of duty, with a message of liberty behind which lurk dark designs: 'il semblait ruminer alors de noirs projets' (p.87). An avatar of the Tempter, he is also the spirit of the absurd and the missing explanation. His first assumed guise is that of 'l'abbé Salus': a homophone of *salut* meaning salvation, and a Latin word which is, ironically, the name of the goddess of the public safety of Rome, as well as meaning health, welfare, good fortune and delivrance from death, all of which, thanks to his interventions, evade Fleurissoire. So, the name is a doorway to salvation or perdition, through which to find or lose one's way. Protos's eyes (see p.226) are agents of spiritual unrest. And his promise of infinite freedom is on a short lease. As with Faust, he returns to reclaim payment, final subservience: 'd'une voix à la fois moqueuse, autoritaire et jubilante, s'écriait: [...] Alors quoi! c'est donc vrai! on avait voulu s'évader?' (p.227). That Protos emerges from his disguise here larger than life, like an evil genie from the bottle, stamps him as symbolic force rather than caricature.

He is the 'Big Brother' figure in the wings, the totalitarian spirit manipulating human destinies, countering individualistic self-expression. One thinks of Baudelaire's 'C'est le Diable qui tient les fils qui nous remuent!' (*Au Lecteur*): never more potent than when preying on the vice of 'Ennui' and its morbid vacuum. Protos is also gangland boss, king of the underworld (in ancient and modern senses), who proves that lawlessness has its own law, perhaps the most unrelenting of all: 'Non, non, Lafcadio, mon ami, non ce n'est pas de l'argent que j'attends de vous; mais de l'obéissance [...] Lafcadio! mon ami, apprenez la loi des subtils' (p.230). As elsewhere, opposites prove to be the same: chance is determinism in disguise, escape imprisons, and the spirit of the centrifugal does not tolerate marginals, eccentrics and freelancers. Though one may think one has escaped Protos's clutches (as after his arrest), he is, like the plague bacillus as symbol of evil in Camus's *La Peste*, ready to re-emerge with a new virulence and victories over him are provisional: 'il se savait peu facile à saisir' (p.239). It is part of the dialectical patterning that, after crying out to God, Amédée gets Lafcadio; and that Lafcadio, after exclaiming 'Diable! diable!' (p.199), gets Protos: the ultimate evil, but also an indispensable source of energy, initiative and invention.

The book goes to the edge of a spiritual void. The phrase 'la disparition de notre chef spirituel' (p.99), while reflecting on characters who all 'lose their spiritual heads', refers to a world where God has, at least temporarily, gone into eclipse. And Protos's words 'Quitter Rome j'ai dit!' (p.98) go beyond the various train journeys, to suggest a more radical departure and disconnection. The result is a spiritual vertigo, if not panic, born of a 'crainte quasi superstitieuse' (p.101). It takes the form, for Amédée, of an existential crisis, in which security gives way to the disorder of physical sensation: a chaos of signals impossible to unscramble. Expulsion from paradise coincides with his plucking from the tree of knowledge and the eating of forbidden fruits: 'Ah! que j'étais heureux quand je ne savais rien, gémit Fleurissoire. Hélas! jamais plus, à présent, je ne pourrai ne pas savoir!' (p.164). Knowledge is irreversible. And what for some might be farewell to false innocence and the road to self-discovery, is for him irretrievable loss. After colds and inflamed skin, he contracts the fundamental sickness: 'La fièvre [...] dont on ne guérit point, et dont on ne veut pas guérir' (p.181). It is a fanatical malady which feeds on itself and becomes, as seen in *La Porte étroite*, a wasting disease: a self-destructive pursuit of Truth in a void, closing the victim in a private passion and severing him from reality. *'There is only one remedy! One thing alone can cure us from being ourselves!'* (p.185), says the epigraph to the fifth and final act. Is that remedy redemption, or simply death? The quotation, while touching the predicaments of Anthime and Amédée ('vous préférez rester malade?' (p.28), asked Véronique), anticipates the deeper metaphysical nihilism which tempts Lafcadio: loss of first freshness with nothing to replace it, universal disinterest (a *reductio ad absurdum* of 'disinterestedness' as indifference to gain), and admission of the absurd. And when Julius speaks of the 'secret effroyable, déconcertant, mais où votre foi, cher Anthime, saura puiser du réconfort' (p.237), it runs counter to a book where the signs indicate a different possibility: that there is 'naught for your comfort'.

Les Caves, like Pandora's box, releases the voices of doubt, including the hypothesis of a dubious God. That so many characters ironically thank God (see pp.113, 148) subverts the word 'ciel'. And the onslaught on heaven crudely done by Anthime, via his science, his blasphemies and his hurled crutch ('il la lance contre le ciel', p.33), is more insidiously pursued by Protos who turns the Lord's name into a mere cipher for his own amusement and gain: 'Pour l'amour du ciel' (p.146), 'Juste ciel!', 'au nom du ciel!' (p.148). The repetition in the later pages of the formula 'Dieu m'est témoin que ...' (pp.235, 236) saps it through over-insistence, making one doubt if God is really witness of anything. Even Julius, finding it all a bit much and operating his own 'interruption de courant', prefers to leave God out of it: 'Ah! ne protestez pas toujours! interrompit de nouveau Julius. – Dieu n'a que faire ici' (p.236). Indeed, does God have anything to do with this book, despite all the religious shenanigans? It is not only 'les faux biens', but the twists and turns of all available routes '[qui] détournent de Dieu' (p.124). And the invisibility of the Pope symbolizes that of a higher authority: the *deus absconditus* who has one running in circles. That Julius should advise Véronique, 'Si vous n'avez rien obtenu, adressez-vous plus haut encore, toujours plus haut' (p.125) is ironic, in that the upward chain of command leads nowhere. It furthers the suspicion that it is at the highest level that the biggest fraud, or broken pact on the part of an author, is being perpetrated: 'Et qui me dira si Fleurissoire en arrivant au paradis n'y découvre pas tout de même que son bon Dieu non plus n'est pas *le vrai*' (p.238).

The title *Les Caves du Vatican* could be translated as the *warnings* of the Vatican. Questions of 'faux dieux' and the ubiquitous exclamation 'ma foi!' are probes into God-substitutes and the credentials of faith. Where, despite curates and cures, does one find true religion? Is it in the trinkets of first communion worn by Julie (p.24), or in the image of Notre-Dame de Lourdes in Arnica's sitting-room, 'en carton-romain, modèle réduit' (p.117), a small-scale patroness for the sedentary? Is it in the clockwork regularity of Amédée's self-protective prayers, as prudent as his purse? Or in the puritan's self-inflicted wound (symbolized by the insect-bite 'qu'il enflammait en se grattant comme à plaisir', p.130), leading not to a religion of joy (the elusive *San Felice*) but to the *gémissement* of the frustrated quest? Is it in a moral rectitude which sees nothing but straight lines and narrow ways? Is it in Julius's politically convenient orthodoxy, hypocritical compromises and ingrowing 'faith' by which he is 'Fidèle [...] à mes pensées, à mes principes' (p.234): true to an unproductive self, with no desire for new investment or redefinition? Is it in the switch-mechanism of Anthime's conversion, turned as easily one way as another, without it making any difference? *Les Caves* is a questioning of gods, and religion is seen, like Protos, in its many travesties: false faces of the faith. Does one then assume that authentic spirituality may be found, not in Church or Vatican, among priests and cardinals or the flock of the faithful, but in unlikely places and barely recognizable as such? Could it, indeed, be in Lafcadio: never drawn into the riddle of Rome and contemptuous of good and evil, but who perhaps embodies the real spiritual quest and, in rejecting crime and punishment, seeks to restore himself (in a way never available to Amédée) to the innocence of a pre-Adamite world?

The spiritual question and that of liberty are synonymous. It is a book, one might say, about 'liberation theology'. The *Croisade pour la délivrance du Pape* (p.141) implies a deeper mission: that of delivering oneself, one's own spiritual 'head', from all that imprisons it in a labyrinth of doubts, impostures and confusions. That salvation is in one's own hands is hinted, albeit through phoney rhetoric, by Protos: 'Quoi! vous avez l'insigne honneur de tenir entre vos mains sa délivrance, et vous tardez!' (p.105). 'Freeing oneself' is a question debated throughout. Lafcadio prizes 'la libre disposition de soi-même' (p.62). But the definition of freedom is not simple or self-evident: it, too, can be a lure, hedged by detours, deviations and dead-ends. *Les Caves du Vatican* might have taken as sub-title Sartre's *Les Chemins de la liberté*: most of them misleading. Anthime's flaunted '*libre* pensée' (p.16) is a compensatory cover-up for major inhibitions, and the product of a blinkered science. Though making himself spokesman of a *morale ouverte* and 'le libre développement de la faculté créatrice' (p.204), Julius's excited question: 'Comprenez-vous ce que veulent dire ces mots: le champ libre?' leads no further than the white page, the padded prison of the literary dilettante. The Lafcadio of the *acte gratuit* is paradoxically 'un homme libre ... à la merci de ...' But he is caught in more subtle dilemmas concerning liberty. Is its essence in spontaneity or self-control, in giving oneself to 'sincere' impulses (which may have their own devious and hypocritical games to play) or in controlling them (which may be a form of self-evasion rather than self-mastery)? Such issues are crystallized in the obsessive presence in the text of the verb 'livrer' and its derivatives (cf. pp.231, 239, 247, 250). From the one Latin stem *liberare*, 'se livrer' can mean to 'deliver/free oneself' (or find deliverance) or to 'deliver oneself up' (or submit/surrender). And there is almost no etymological distance between 'un homme libre' and 'un homme qui se livre', despite the contrasting translations. Again, the same can produce its opposite, and one treads the fine border of freedom and imprisonment masquerading as the same, sharing a common authorship or paternity, and swopping disguises almost unnoticed.

The underground threat to liberty comes to a climax in the encounter between Protos and Lafcadio. Here, matters of integrity and compromise, and the pious ideal of 'l'homme sincère' (p.204), are put to their severest test. So many of his possessions have been appropriated that Lafcadio has had cause to doubt what he can call his own. Now Protos, in his 'true' colours, makes the ultimate take-over bid: 'Lafcadio, mon ami, soyez raisonnable; vous soumettez-vous?' (p.231). What irony that the grasping Protos, alias l'abbé Salus, should have said, with a sickly perversion of the word 'integrity': 'Les gens intègres exigent l'intégralité' (p.104)! What people are subservient to – fears, creeds, social prejudices – has been a central theme. Now, for an 'in-between' Lafcadio ('entre deux âges'), the crunch comes: will he be the slave of the 'liberator' once idealized? Protos's bleak pragmatic message is that there can be no half-measures, no fence-sitting (one recalls Gide's statement on the unacceptability of both protestantism and catholicism): 'Mais ce qui m'étonne, moi, c'est que, intelligent comme vous êtes, vous ayez cru, Cadio, qu'on pouvait si simplement que ça sortir d'une société, et sans tomber du même coup dans une autre' (p.230). The adolescent who played with dice, kept options open and left room for manoeuvre, is forced up against choices. Protos's voice offers no escape-routes and no exceptions. Law and lawlessness are equally totalitarian states and, whichever one chooses, one must obey the rules of the game. It is the voice of moral blackmail, writ large, to which Gide was sensitive throughout his life: ultimatums to belong to one camp or the other, coercive pressures to conform. Protos's trump-card is the threat to sell Lafcadio ('le livrer') to the police, in terms starkly simple: physical imprisonment by the law, or imprisonment in the regimented structures of criminal gangland – 'Désormais vous dépendez d'elle – ou de nous' (p.231). Opposites, once more, show the same face: though hating rebels, the police collaborate with the underworld, and vice versa, in maintaining a workable status quo. 'Je suis un peu de la police, mon garçon. J'ai l'œil. J'aide au bon ordre' (ibid.), says Protos. Observing that Lafcadio has already 'sold out' and become the lap-dog of

Baraglioul wealth, he makes his own offer seem a return to greater integrity; and he beckons his ex-playmate into the chain of blackmail, proposing that *he* should now put the squeeze on Julius, saying 'Le chantage est une saine institution, nécessaire au maintien des mœurs' (p.232), typically distorting a vice into a virtue.

The 'temptation' of Lafcadio does not end here. Having said 'Get thee behind me, Satan' and left the compartment (striding over Protos's outstretched legs through 'la porte du couloir', just as Protos (p.142) stepped over Carola through an invisible door in what seemed an impenetrable wall or impasse), Lafcadio will run the gauntlet of tempting voices, all saying implicitly 'give yourself up'. In this penultimate phase, Gide (who has laid bait for him throughout) hastens the play of confrontational duets: Protos – Julius – Geneviève. And, each time, the lad is more susceptible: disenchantment in the aftermath of the *acte gratuit* before meeting Protos, resignation and 'le sentiment de sa dépendance' (p.241) before meeting Julius, tears of rejection and self-pity before meeting Geneviève. Gide also, in this three-stage battle for the 'soul' of Lafcadio, keeps the pendulum swinging to and fro. The call to join outlaws and agents of 'le Malin' is followed by Julius's call to join social respectability and (in a sermon like that first delivered to Anthime) the succour of the Church. But here, too, opposites are one: in that both stand for order and conformity, and both advocate moral compromise (with Julius ironically urging, 'Allons; mon garçon, un peu de courage: allez vous confesser' (p.244), where 'go to confession' means 'do not confess to the police' and the appeal for courage is the symptom of his own moral cowardice). The final visitation from a would-be 'redeemer' is that of Geneviève. In Lafcadio's Italian journey between Scylla and Charybdis, where Protos was the whirlpool (movement and vertigo), Geneviève is the rock (the dream of stability). Her siren's tones, coupled with the lure of virginal beauty and selfless devotion, repeat, family-fashion, what Julius has said, but with truer religious conviction: 'C'est à Dieu qu'il faut vous livrer, non aux hommes' and 'l'Eglise est là [...] pour vous aider à retrouver la paix, par-delà votre repentir' (pp.247-48). She offers to salvage what she sees, naïvely, as Lafcadio's 'better self' (the heroic, altruistic self apparent in the rescue of the child) and rehabilitate him through love.

As with the 'Will he? Won't he?' of Anthime's spiritual cliff-hanger, the narrator delights in suspense. He toys with our expectations, taking the side of realism and moral orthodoxy, and appearing to concur with the defeatist message of Protos and the logic of the 'impasse' ('vous soumettez-vous?'): 'Geneviève a raison; et certes Lafcadio n'a rien de mieux à faire qu'une commode soumission; il l'éprouvera tôt ou tard, et que les autres issues sont bouchées' (p.248). Yet, within a page, he (or his near-identical twin the author) will fling the doors of the novel open, in a fanfare of liberty and possibility, so performing his own escapologist's trick and, throwing off the borrowed rhetorical face, show himself to be, no less than Lafcadio, an 'être d'inconséquence'. And, having tempted *us* with a conventional happy ending (with all the romantic accompaniments of a Mills and Boon, the sweet caress of his breath, a feverish brow, her hair and will falling undone, sighed names in the half-light), an ending which, he hints, will dispel once and for all the false dreams and pretences which have clouded their young lives, the author switches direction yet again in the very last lines. To the kisses and embraces, he first adds his own enthusiastic *envoi*: 'Ici commence un nouveau livre. / O vérité palpable du désir; tu repousses dans la pénombre les fantômes de mon esprit' (p.249) – as if he, too, has suffered from illusions and is now, at the end of a confused journey, clarifying his own perspectives; as if, in this book which has hovered between truth and falsity, he can at last give credence, amidst the deceptive values, to the reality and reliability of young love. And, in a text where fiction and real life have been un-comfortable bedfellows, the *livre* and *vérité* now seem to come together, happily reconciled. But the final sentence of the *sotie* – 'Quoi! va-t-il renoncer à vivre? et pour l'estime de Geneviève, qu'il estime un peu moins depuis qu'elle l'aime un peu plus, songe-t-il encore à se livrer?' (p.250) – disconcertingly changes tack. For, as Lafcadio gazes through 'la fenêtre grande ouverte', it is towards a dawn unlikely to include Geneviève, whose now-discarded body he literally overlooks. So the text, which has exploited throughout the discrepancy between expectation and event, stays true to itself in its infidelity. It cannot resist one final about-turn and change of face, jilting the attractions of what it has just so lyrically fashioned, so that the love-idyll ('ces paupières nacrées, ces lèvres chaudes entrouvertes, ces seins parfaits') is also discarded and passes like a dream, a moment's false intoxicant. The 'vérité palpable du désir', indubitable at one minute, is itself 'repoussée dans la pénombre'. And, in a book where characters coincide and diverge again, Geneviève and Lafcadio, drawn tantalizingly close (with common feelings and echoing words), seem doomed to go their separate ways.

Is it that, for Gide, there is no salvation *à deux*? The message of individualism emerges unscathed. Lafcadio, who has seen cuff-links, hat and *acte gratuit* disappearing in someone else's hands, is not ready to give *himself* to Geneviève, Julius or Protos. Where others weaken, he ultimately has the courage to 'go it alone'. ('Tous contre soi!' (p.163), Protos warned Amédée.) And where, for Julius, the words 'porte ouverte' mean mouldering in the stuffiness of the Académie and, for Amédée, demise through the carriage door, two dead ends, for Lafcadio they represent genuine departure, the insatiable instinct for elsewheres. Having stepped over Protos and opened the door, he is now poised to pass beyond Geneviève (the watchword 'PASSER OUTRE' retains its energy) and look through a window which no longer encloses or stifles (cf. p.248), but admits the sensual tremor and *élan vital* of a fresh dawn. It is significant that the clarion call, the reveille, is heard from 'les casernes', places of collective enclosure and regimentation. It carries, therefore, a message of escape and liberation. Whereas others retreat to the shelter of communal life, following the moral that '*Il ne faut jamais ôter le retour à personne*' (p.43), Lafcadio is turned only to futures. So he is the living contradiction of the words: 'Hors la Maison, point de salut pour toi' (*1*, p.480); and upholds Gide's statement: 'Je suis, tu sais, de rédemption difficile, et contrecarre les desseins des Sauveurs!' [7] The last word of the text is the verb 'se livrer?', in interrogative form. Lafcadio, certainly, does not surrender. 'Il se dé-

---

[7] *Correspondance Gide-Jammes*, Gallimard, 1948, p.117.

livre': frees himself, literally, from the prison of the book. 'Ne pas s'enfermer dans sa seule vie',[8] one reads in *Les Cahiers d'André Walter*. While other characters, having died, been arrested or shut up shop, stay closed in the purgatory of the text, Lafcadio alone crosses the threshold to a new story, still unformulated. His future is not written in the past. He is available for a new series, with all its unpredictabilities. Typically, the author, as he has done at the end of each individual part of the *sotie*, now, at the end of the book as a whole, breaks with what has preceded and, as an *être d'inconséquence*, releases us to new developments. 'Je sens mille possibles en moi; mais je ne puis me résigner à n'en vouloir être qu'un seul' (*2*, p.28), wrote Gide; and 'Je ne suis jamais; je deviens' (*2*, p.830). Lafcadio leaves us with his *disponibilité* intact. What was for Amédée a mortal fever and the agonies of the Cross becomes, for Lafcadio, endless fervour and infinite crossroads. He is rejuvenated, not by taking Geneviève's virginity, but by rediscovering his own. And the final note rejoins that of *Les Nourritures terrestres* (1897): inexhaustible appetite for the newness of the world.

At the same time, the novel finds its own salvation: 'Ici commence un nouveau livre'. It rejects the temptation to acquire a past. Like Lafcadio, it is a phoenix reborn from its ashes. It shakes off its own 'torpeur', its own temptation towards the calm of resolution. It keeps its options open to the very last, not only by toying with expectations, but by defying the momentum of its own directions. In a literary context so concerned with openings and closures, it proves that (unlike the 'impasse Claude-Bernard') it is not a dead-end. It does not have to submit to the gloomy determinism, the message of inevitability, of a literary Protos, or to acknowledge that freedom was, all along, imprisonment in disguise. In this book of 'transgressions', Gide has unashamedly broken the boundaries of narrative role, self-contained characterization and linguistic parochialism. Now the book 'transgresses itself', steps beyond its own finitude, refuses to become an end in itself. The *envoi* of *Les Nourritures terrestres*, addressed to the ideal imagined

---

[8] Gallimard, 1952, p.35.

and the work as a whole is described by Gide as 'ce manuel d'évasion, de délivrance' (*1*, pp.248-49). *Les Caves* delivers itself from the evils of self-satisfaction and closure. It not only carries a message of liberty, but *embodies* it in its final determination to 'PASSER OUTRE'. In so doing, and whether going by the name of *sotie* or any other alias, it rejoins its own true self: the novel as *novel*: infinite newness, forms beyond forms.

Select Bibliography

For more complete bibliographical information on Gide, one should consult C. Martin, *La Maturité d'André Gide*, Klincksieck, 1972, and the frequent updatings provided by *Les Cahiers d'André Gide* 1969-, and by *La Revue des Lettres Modernes: André Gide* 1970-, with its separately published 'carnets bibliographiques'.

CENTRAL EDITIONS OF GIDE'S MAJOR WRITINGS

1. André Gide, *Romans, récits et soties, œuvres lyriques*, Paris, Gallimard, 'Bibliothèque de la Pléiade', 1958
2. ——, *Journal 1889-1939*, Paris, Gallimard, 'Bibliothèque de la Pléiade', 1948
3. ——, *Journal 1939-1949*, Paris, Gallimard, 'Bibliothèque de la Pléiade', 1954

CRITICAL WORKS INDISPENSABLE FOR THE STUDY OF *LES CAVES DU VATICAN*

4. Bettinson, Christopher, *Gide: Les Caves du Vatican*, London, Edward Arnold, 'Studies in French Literature' 20, 1972
5. Fillaudeau, Bertrand, *L'Univers ludique d'André Gide: les soties*, Paris, Corti, 1985
6. Goulet, Alain, *Les Caves du Vatican d'André Gide: étude méthodologique*, Paris, Larousse, 1972

FURTHER READING

7. Atkinson, John K., '*Les Caves du Vatican* and Bergson's *Le Rire*', *Publications of the Modern Language Association*, LXXXIV, 2 (March 1969), pp.328-35
8. Bancroft, W. Jane, '*Les Caves du Vatican*: vers l'écriture du roman', *Revue des Lettres Modernes*, André Gide 6 (1979), pp.159-75
9. Bastide, Roger, *Anatomie d'André Gide*, Paris, Presses Universitaires de France, 1972

10. Batchelor, R.E., 'Gide et Unamuno: sotie ou nivola?', *Nottingham French Studies*, IX, 1 (May 1970), pp.44-53
11. Bell, W.M.L., 'Convention and plausibility in *Les Caves du Vatican*', *Australian Journal of French Studies*, VII, 1-2 (January/August 1970), pp.76-92
12. Brée, Germaine, 'Time sequences and consequences in the Gidian world', *Yale French Studies*, VII (1951), pp.51-59
13. ——, *André Gide, l'insaisissable Protée*, Paris, Les Belles Lettres, 1953
14. ——, '*Les Caves du Vatican*', *L'Esprit créateur*, 1 (1961), pp.9-13
15. Cancalon, Elaine D., 'La structure du système dans *Les Caves du Vatican*', *Revue des Lettres Modernes*, André Gide 7 (1984), pp.117-44
16. ——, 'De Lafcadio à Bernard: l'adaptation de l'inadapté', *Revue des Lettres Modernes*, André Gide 8 (1987), pp.75-86
17. Davet, Yvonne, 'Notice sur *Les Caves du Vatican*' in André Gide, *Romans (see 1)*, pp.1565-71
18. Delorme, Cécile, 'Narcissisme et éducation dans l'œuvre romanesque de Gide', *Etudes gidiennes*, 1 (1970), pp.91-109
19. Faurisson, Robert, '*Les Caves du Vatican*: essai d'explication à l'usage des élèves et des étudiants', *L'Information littéraire*, XVIII, 3 (May/June 1966), pp.124-30
20. Fernandez, Ramon, *André Gide*, Paris, Corrêa, 1931 (republished by Klincksieck in 'Bibliothèque du XXe siècle', 1985)
21. Freyburger, Henri, *L'Evolution de la disponibilité gidienne*, Paris, Nizet, 1970
22. Geracht, M. Aron, 'A guide through the Vatican caves: a study of the structure of *Les Caves du Vatican*', *Wisconsin Studies in Contemporary Literature*, VI, 3 (Autumn 1965), pp.330-45
23. Goulet, Alain, 'L'Ecriture de l'acte gratuit', *Revue des Lettres Modernes*, André Gide 6 (1979), pp.177-201
24. Grieve, James A., 'Lafcadio: a reappraisal', *Australian Journal of French Studies*, III, 1 (January/April 1966), pp.22-35
25. Guérard, Albert, *André Gide*, New York, Dutton, 1969
26. Holdheim, William W., 'Gide's *Les Caves du Vatican* and the illusionism of the novel', *Modern Language Notes*, LXXVII, 3 (May 1962), pp.292-304
27. Ireland, G.W., *André Gide, a study of his creative writings*, Oxford, Clarendon Press, 1970
28. Jones, F.J., Introduction and Notes to edition of *Les Caves du Vatican*, University of London Press, 1961, pp.9-39, 225-33
29. Lafille, Pierre, *André Gide romancier*, Paris, Hachette, 1954

30. Maisani-Léonard, M., *André Gide ou l'ironie de l'écriture*, Montreal University Press, 1976
31. Martin, Claude, *André Gide par lui-même*, Paris, Seuil, 1963
32. ——, 'Gide et le nouveau roman', *Entretiens sur André Gide*, Mouton, Centre de Cerisy-la-Salle, 1967
33. Marty, Eric, *André Gide: Qui êtes-vous?*, Lyon, La Manufacture, 1987
34. Niemeyer, Carl, 'Raskolnikov and Lafcadio', *Modern Fiction Studies*, IV, 3 (Autumn 1958), pp.253-61
35. O'Brien, Justin, 'Gide's fictional technique', *Yale French Studies*, VII (1951), pp.81-90
36. ——, 'Lafcadio and Barnabooth, a supposition', *Symposium*, VIII, 1 (1954), pp.33-41
37. O'Neill, Kevin, *André Gide and the roman d'aventures*, Sydney University Press, 1969
38. Pandolfo, M., 'La démystification du paraître dans *Les Caves du Vatican*', *Bulletin des amis d'André Gide*, 39, pp.49-57
39. Sonnenfeld, Albert, 'De Dostoievski à Gide', *Cahiers André Gide*, 3 (1972), pp.341-50
40. Steel, D.A., 'Gide and the conception of the bastard', *French Studies*, XVII, 3 (July 1963), pp.238-48
41. ——, 'Le Prodigue chez Gide: essai de critique économique de l'acte gratuit', *Revue d'histoire littéraire de la France*, LXX, 2 (March/April 1970), pp.209-29
42. ——, ' "Lafcadio ludens": ideas of play and levity in *Les Caves du Vatican*', *Modern Language Review*, LXVI, 3 (July 1971), pp.254-64
43. Strauss, George, 'The original Juste-Agénor: an unpublished fragment of *Les Caves du Vatican*', *Australian Journal of French Studies*, III, 1 (January/April 1966), pp.9-15
44. Watson, Graeme, 'Protos', *Australian Journal of French Studies*, III, 1 (January/April 1966), pp.16-21
45. York, Ruth, 'Circular patterns in Gide's *Soties*', *French Review*, XXXIV, 4 (February 1961), pp.336-43

INTERACTIVE READING

To an interviewer who said that he could not see the essential difference between *Les Caves du Vatican* and *Les Faux-Monnayeurs*, Gide replied: 'Il n'y en a peut-être pas, en effet. Peut-être était-ce encore une illusion de ma part' (see *33*, p.250). With this in mind, the study of *Les Faux-Monnayeurs* by Michael Tilby, in the present series of critical guides, cannot be too highly recommended, together with its complementary bibliography.

CRITICAL GUIDES TO FRENCH TEXTS

edited by
Roger Little, Wolfgang van Emden, David Williams